Species of Protallocoxoidea and Stenetrioidea (Isopoda, Asellota) From the Antarctic and Southern Seas

George A. Schultz

Arcturidae From the Antarctic and Southern Seas (Isopoda, Valvifera), Part 1

George A. Schultz

Papers 2 and 3 in

Biology of the Antarctic Seas X
Antarctic Research Series Volume 32

Louis S. Kornicker, Editor

American Geophysical Union

Paper 2
SPECIES OF PROTALLOCOXOIDEA AND
STENETRIOIDEA (ISOPODA, ASELLOTA)
FROM THE ANTARCTIC AND SOUTHERN
SEAS
GEORGE A. SCHULTZ
Page 17

Paper 3
ARCTURIDAE FROM THE ANTARCTIC AND
SOUTHERN SEAS (ISOPODA, VALVIFERA)
PART 1
GEORGE A. SCHULTZ
Page 63

BIOLOGY OF THE ANTARCTIC SEAS X
Antarctic Research Series Volume 32

LOUIS S. KORNICKER, Editor

Published under the aegis of the
Board of Associate Editors, Antarctic Research Series
Charles R. Bentley, Chairman
Robert H. Eather, David H. Elliot, Dennis E. Hayes
Louis S. Kornicker, Heinz H. Lettau, and Bruce C. Parker

Library of Congress Cataloging in Publication Data

Schultz, George A.
  Species of Protallocoxoidea and Stenetrioidea (Isopoda,
Assellota) from the Antarctic and Southern seas ; Arcturi-
dae from the Antarctic and Southern seas (Isopoda,
Valvifera)

  (Papers 2 and 3 in Biology of the Antarctic Seas ; 10)
(Antarctic research series ; v. 32)
  Bibliography: p.
  1. Protallocoxidae. 2. Stenetriidae. 3. Arcturidae.
4. Crustacea—Antarctic regions. 5. Eltanin (Ship)
I. Title. II. Title: Arcturidae from the Antarctic
and southern seas (Isopoda, Valvifera) III. Title:
Protallocoxoidea and Stenetrioidea (Isopoda, Asellota)
from the Antarctic and Southern seas. IV. Title:
Stenetrioidea (Isopoda, Asellota) from the Antarctic and
Southern seas. V. Series: Biology of the Antarctic
Seas ; 10, papers 2–3. VI. Series: Antarctic research
series ; v. 32.
QH95.58.B56 vol. 10, papers 2–3 [QL444.M34]   81-14981
ISBN 0-87590-178-6   574.92′4s   AACR2
                         [595.3′72]

Published by the
AMERICAN GEOPHYSICAL UNION
With the aid of grant DPP-7721859 from the
National Science Foundation
February 10, 1982

Printed in the United States of America

SPECIES OF PROTALLOCOXOIDEA AND STENETRIOIDEA (ISOPODA, ASELLOTA) FROM THE ANTARCTIC AND SOUTHERN SEAS

George A. Schultz

Hampton, New Jersey 08827

Abstract. Species of the superfamilies Protallocoxoidea Schultz [1978] and Stenetrioidea Wolff [1962], of the suborder Asellota, from the Antarctic and southern seas are discussed. A second species of Protallocoxoidea is described from off the southern tip of South America. The genus Stenetrium Haswell [1881] and the type species S. armatum Haswell are redescribed. Specimens of Stenetriidae from Antarctica, Australia, New Zealand, and South Africa are redescribed or discussed, a total of 25 species of the genus south of the Tropic of Capricorn thus being reviewed. One of the 25 species is described in a new genus, and a previously described species is placed in a new genus. Three genera then are included in the formerly monogeneric family Stenetriidae.

Introduction

Species of two superfamilies, Protallocoxoidea Schultz [1978] and Stenetrioidea Wolff [1962], of the suborder Asellota from the Antarctic and southern seas, are discussed here. The superfamily Protallocoxoidea is based on Protallocoxa weddellensis Schultz [1978]. A second species of the genus is described here. Stenetrioidea is based on Stenetrium armatum Haswell [1881] from eastern Australia, and that species, as well as the genus, is redescribed here. Four other species from Australia also are discussed. In addition, one species from New Zealand and nine from South Africa, including two new species and one in a new genus, are diagnosed, redescribed, or fully described. All species previously recorded from the Antarctic and southern seas are discussed and briefly redescribed, and five new ones, one in a new genus of Stenetriidae, are described. A total of 25 species of Stenetriidae, 23 in Stenetrium Haswell and 2 in new genera, are then included here from the Antarctic and southern seas. Specimens from the Australian Museum (Sydney) and the University of Cape Town Museum, Republic of South Africa, were examined for this study. A diagnosis and a brief or full description are included for all species of Stenetriidae from south of the Tropic of Capricorn. The distribution of all of the species is recorded on Map 1, and a summary of the species and of the disposition of type specimens is given in the appendix. The following abbreviations have been used in the text: AM, Australian Museum; UCT, University of Cape Town Museum.

Superfamily PROTALLOCOXOIDEA Schultz

Schultz [1978] defined the superfamily on the basis of the particular morphology of the coxae on peraeonal segment I of a specimen from the Weddell Sea off Antarctica. The coxal segments are free, not fused, at the ends of peraeonal segment I. This condition is unique among the Asellota, although it is present on species of Plakarthriidae, of the suborder Flabellifera. Schultz [1979] discussed the relationship of Protallocoxoidea to Plakarthriidae and pointed out its implications to the evolution of the Asellota and Flabellifera.

Family PROTALLOCOXIDEA Schultz
Protallocoxa Schultz

Protallocoxa weddellensis Schultz [1978] has been the type species and the only species in the genus until now. Unfortunately, the new species, like P. weddellensis, is based on a female, and males are not known for either species of the genus. The species of the genus have free coxae or epimeres on peraeonal segment I (Figure 1B).

Protallocoxa drakensis n. sp.
Figs. 1A-1I

Diagnosis. Eyes of about 18 ocelli; coxal extensions project out beyond edges of peraeonal segment IV.

Description. Eyes well developed and of about 18 ocelli. Frontal margin of cephalon with acutely pointed anterolateral and frontal processes each of which projects forward about same length. Rostrum shorter than broad; rostrum pointed. Cephalon narrower than width of peraeonal segment I and free coxal segments; coxal segments with pointed anterolateral projection. Peraeonal segments II and III wider than all others. Coxal extensions extend from large notches on posterolateral corners on segment IV. Peraeonal segment V narrowest and shortest with subquadrate lateral borders. Pleon with two free segments. Pleotelson narrower

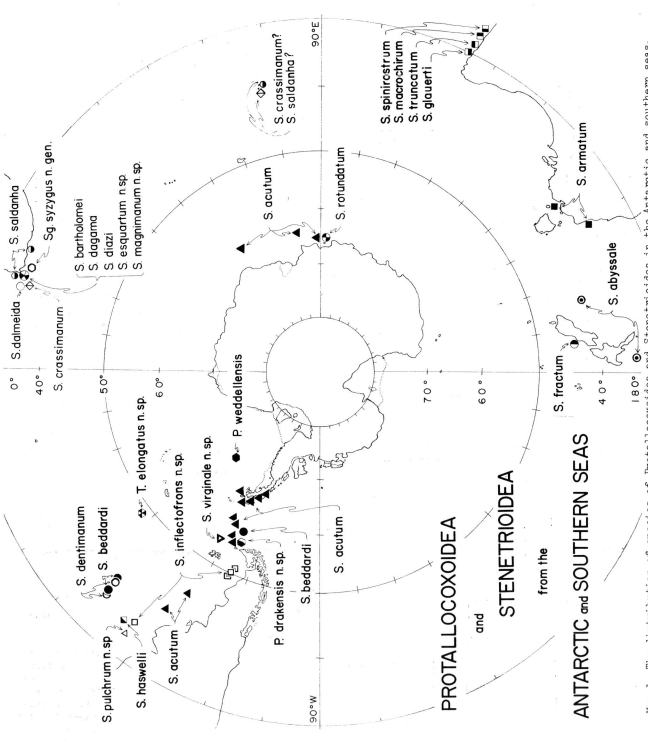

Map 1. The distribution of species of Protallocoxoidea and Stenetrioidea in the Antarctic and southern seas.

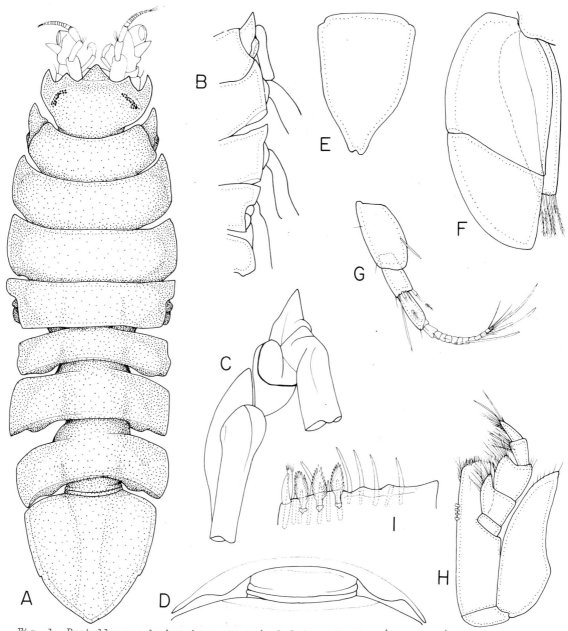

Fig. 1. *Protallocoxa drakensis* n. sp.: A, holotype female, (9 mm long); B, detail, edges of anterior peraeonal segments; C, detail, undersides of segments I and II; D, anterior part, pleon; E, female pleopod 2 (sympod); F, pleopod 3; G, antenna 1; H, maxilliped; I, detail, sensory edge of endite of maxilliped.

than peraeonal segment VII with gradually narrowing lateral margins and pointed posterior margin. Posterolateral notches on pleotelson minute. Pleopod 2 (sympod) with notch on narrowed posterior edge. Antenna 1 with 13 flagellar articles.

Measurements. Holotype female, 9 mm long; paratype juvenile, 4.5 mm long.

Type locality. Hero station 715-895; approximately 25 km south of Isla de los Estados, Tierra del Fuego, Argentina; start at 54°59.9'S, 64°50'W; 438 m; finish at 55°00'S, 64°47.5'W; 548 m; November 3, 1971.

Affinities. The new species differs from P. weddellensis Schultz, the only other species in the genus, in that the eyes are larger, the rostrum is shorter, and the coxal extensions are visible in dorsal view on segment IV. In addition, the posterolateral notches on the pleotelson are minute, not small, and the edges of the cephalon, peraeonal segments, and pleotelson are smooth and without the tiny serrulations which are present in P. weddellensis. It is also similar to Stenetrium beddardi Kussakin [1967], but Kussakin makes no mention of any free coxal segments on peraeonal segment I.

Remarks. The new sepcies is from off the southern tip of the South American continent well north of the Antarctic convergence, whereas P. weddellensis is from the Weddell Sea south of the convergence near the Antarctic continent.

Superfamily STENETRIOIDEA Wolff
Family STENETRIIDAE Hansen

The genus Stenetrium was instituted by Haswell [1881], who described and illustrated two species, S. armatum and S. inerme, from eastern Australia. He essentially repeated the descriptions later [Haswell, 1882]. In a third publication, Haswell [1885] described a difference in peraeopod I and antenna 2 between males and females but did not mention differences in the rostrum or anterior edge of the cephalon. Hansen [1905] published a summary and revision of the species of Stenetrium, including five new ones and four described by others [Chilton, 1884; Beddard, 1886a, b; Richardson, 1902]. Although Hansen redescribed the two species of Haswell, he mentioned that S. inerme was not a Stenetrium but rather that it 'agree[d] much more with the same parts in males belonging to a genus allied to Ianira.' However, he did not name the allied genus. Schultz [1976] discussed its morphology and placed it in Iathrippa Bovallius. Thus of the two species described by Haswell, only the type species, S. armatum, was formally included in Hansen's revision, redescription, and redefinition of the nine species of the genus. Since Stebbing [1905] described a new species, there were 10 species in Stenetrium Haswell in 1905.

Nobili [1906] briefly described two species from the Îles Tuamotu of the southern Pacific, and later [Nobili, 1907] he more fully described them and added a new one. Vanhöffen [1914] described two species from the Antarctic Sea. Barnard [1914] added one species to the genus and later [Barnard, 1920] added four more, all from South Africa. Nicholls [1929] added four species from western Australia. Monod [1933] redescribed S. chiltoni Stebbing, but Nordenstam [1946] later called it a new species, S. monodi. Barnard [1940] added two new species from South Africa. Miller [1941] added one from Hawaii, and Nordenstam [1946] added two from the Gilbert Islands. Wolff [1962] described a species from the Kermadec Trench northeast of New Zealand, and Kussakin [1967] added two species from the South Atlantic and added to the distribution records of species from Antarctic seas. Menzies and Glynn [1968] added a species from Puerto Rico and extended the range of two others from the Virgin Islands to that island. Kensley [1975] added a 'Stenetrium

sp.' from Still Bay, South Africa. With the addition of five more species here, the total number of species in Stenetrium Haswell, including those from the northern locations, is now 38. If Kensley's 'Stenetrium sp.' is a distinct species, then the number is 39.

The distinct morphology of the pleonal appendages of members of the genus, along with a summary of the species from North American waters, was included by Schultz [1969, p. 238]. Stenetrium Haswell is now redescribed.

Description of genus. Eyes of few or many ocelli. Body dorsoventrally compressed, generally about one third as wide as it is long. Anterolateral margins of cephalon usually sharply pointed; frontal processes usually present. Rostrum on frontal margin of cephalon variously shaped (rectangular or triangular), with frontal margin truncate, rounded, or pointed. Peraeonal segments I-IV with anterolateral margins pointed; coxae generally visible in dorsal view on some, sometimes on all four. Slight indications of coxal suture on lateral part of peraeonal segment I on some species. Peraeonal segments V-VII with anterolateral angles pointed; posterolateral angles rounded, with coxae visible on posterior margin (dorsal view) of each. Large female specimens and most males with sternal keels on all segments. Pleotelson shield shaped, usually with posterolateral notches and spines; posterior margin rounded or pointed.

Antenna 1 much shorter than length of body with several to many flagellar articles. Antenna 2 as long as, or longer than, length of body with six (proximal one can be obscured) peduncular articles and multiarticulate flagellum. Antennal scale (squama) present on peduncular article 3. Mandible with toothed incisor process, blunt well-developed molar process, and many setae in setal row. Mandibular palp triarticulate with curved especially setose apical article. Left mandible with lacinia mobilis. Maxilla 1 with many large spines on exopod and two or three spines on endopod. Outer and medial branches of maxilla 2 with three to five large spines; inner wider branch with many large spines. In addition to large spines all branches with many thin hairlike spines. Maxilliped with three to six coupling hooks; apical two palp articles narrower than proximal three articles; exopod generally pointed apically.

Male and female peraeopods I with expanded propodus; male's especially well developed. Peraeopod I of male with palm of propodus variously modified, with different bladelike extensions on edge; propodus of female generally straight with row of long setae on edge. Peraeopods II-VII with two claws on dactyli. Male pleopods 1 about one-half length of pleopods 3 with fused bases and two semicircular segments set above pleopod 2. Basis of pleopod 2 elongated with endopod (folded inwardly) and exopod on distal medial margin. Pleopods 3 operculate to branchial cavity; exopod biarticulate; endopod about half as wide as exopod. Pleopod 4 with single segment of endopod and biarticulato oxopod. Pleopod 5 generally of one segment (exopod) [Hansen, 1905]. Uropods biramous, exopod shorter than uropod, both usually elongate and apically pointed. Uropod generally visible in dorsal view.

Etymology and gender. 'Sten,' from the Greek stenos, means narrow, and 'etr,' from etron, means abdomen; thus the name denotes narrow abdomen. The gender is neuter.

Type species. Stenetrium armatum Hasell [1881].

Remarks. Purely generic characters will not be included in the description of the new species which follow. The new species and some of those previously described also will be compared to S. armatum Haswell (type species), which is redescribed here. The species from the Antarctic and southern seas, except for S. armatum, will be described in alphabetical order, and then the new species from the region will be described.

Stenetrium armatum Haswell
Figs. 2A-2J, 3A-3M, and 4A-4E

Stenetrium armatum Haswell, 1881, p. 478, pl. 19, fig. 1; 1882, p. 308; 1885, p. 1009, pl. 51, figs. 1-12.--Whitelegge, 1889, p. 222.--Hansen, 1905, p. 318, pl. 19, figs. 1a-1d.--Hale, 1929, p. 324, fig. 328.--Wolff, 1962, p. 23.

Diagnosis. Especially long anterolateral corners of cephalon and shape of manus on male peraeopod I unique.

Description. Eyes reniform, of about 18 ocelli. Body elongate, dorsoventrally flattened, and with moderate amount of hairlike setae. Lateral edges subparallel, widest (only slightly) at peraeonal segments I and II. Cephalon with moderately long pointed anterolateral processes; frontal margin with short obtuse frontal processes. Rostrum various, from short and pointed (Figure 4C) to short and subquadrate (truncate) to moderately long and broadly rounded (Figure 2A). (Configuration of rostrum not sexually dimorphic as illustrations in literature suggest.)

Anterolateral edges of peraeonal segments I-IV pointed anteriorly; I most pointed and longest, II-IV each progressively less pointed. Peraeonal segments V-VII about half length of segment I. Coxal plates visible in dorsal view on segments I, II, and IV. Posterolateral edges of segments V-VII progressively more acutely pointed. Coxal processes visible dorsally on segments V-VII. Ventral keels moderately developed on sterna of peraeonal segments of large specimens.

Pleon with two free segments plus pleotelson. Length of pleotelson almost equal to width; lateral edges lightly serrated, posterolateral spines moderately large. Posterior margin of pleotelson evenly rounded; uropods set in shallow notches.

Antenna 1 shorter than width of cephalon, with three peduncular segments visible (dorsal view); article 1 of flagellum very short, half hidden by oblique apical margin of segment 3. Flagellar

article 2 slightly longer than three of next approximately 11 articles. Many sensory setae variously placed on peduncular segments; one aesthetasc on each flagellar article; several on apical article. Antenna 2 with large lateral spine on peduncular segment 1; small nonspined segment 2. Segment 3 with scoop-shaped scale, a squama, placed in obliquely slanted apical edge; squama about as long as segment is wide. Small nonspined segment 4; segments 5 and 6 subequal in length, together about as long as combined peduncular segments 1-4.

Manus of peraeopod I in male with propodus longer than wide; palm with larger terminal spine and large bladelike processes on edge. Dactylus, with very fine toothed setae on inner edge, extending about one quarter of length beyond large terminal palmar spine. Dorsal edge of merus moderately produced. Basis about as long as propodus. Manus of peraeopod I of female with small bladelike expansion on inner edge; small terminal palmar spine and many very small toothed spines on palm. Dactylus only slightly longer than palm. Manus with outer edge produced distally. Male and female peraeopod I covered with many long hairlike setae.

Peraeopod II of male and female with two subequal apical claws and one inferior dactyl claw. Peraeopods III-VII very much alike; all with three claws.

Uropods much shorter than pleotelson; basis shorter than exopod; endopod longer than exopod. Apical setae present on rami and marginal setae present on rami and basis of uropod.

Labrum rounded, with many short sensory bristles and scales. Right mandible with four teeth on incisor process. Eleven setae in setal row and molar process blunt, toothed, and with several setae. Left mandible with five incisor teeth; lacinia mobilis with three teeth and one seta; five setae in setal row; molar process blunt, toothed, and with setae. Palp triarticulate, article 1 shortest and with several hairlike setae; article 2 longest, fringed on inner margin with many small setae and two large toothed setae. Apical article spoon shaped, with large setae on margins and with longest curved and toothed setae at apex. Hypopharynx with simple lobed structure fringed with short setae on apex and shorter setae on inner margin.

Maxilla 1 with exopod with about 11 spines, many denticulate; endopod with two large spines and one small setaceous spine. Outer blade of maxilla 2 with six large comblike spines; middle one with six (four very long) comblike spines; and inner blade shortest, about twice as wide as other two blades, and with at least six large comblike spines on inner margins and at least four on apex. All blades amply provided with setae on inner margins. Maxilliped with widest (article 3) of five palp articles over half as wide as endite. Right and left endites with five coupling hooks on medial edges. Exopod slightly narrower and shorter than endite and with pointed apexes and evenly spaced short setae on inner apical margin.

Male pleopods 1 about one-quarter length of ple-

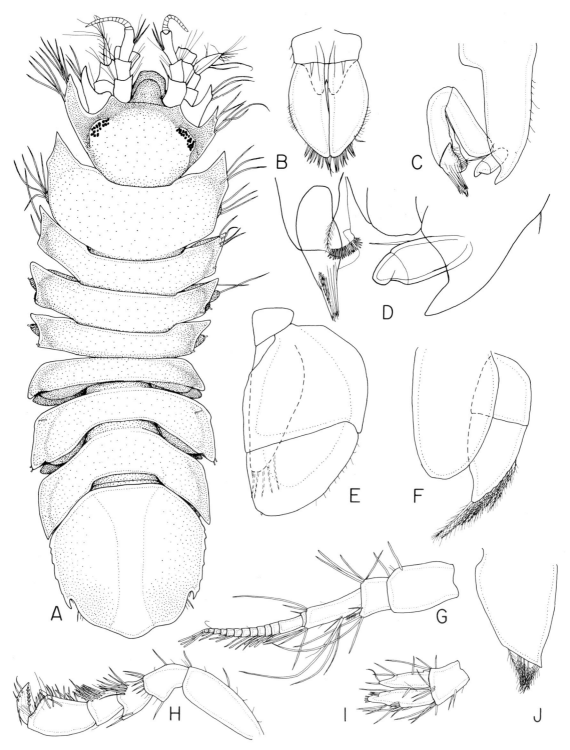

Fig. 2. _Stenetrium armatum_ Haswell, 1881: A, male (6.2 mm long); B and C, male pleopods 1 and 2, respectively; D, detail, male pleopod 2; E and F, pleopods 3 and 4,
respectively; G, antenna 1; H, female peraeopod I, uropod; J, pleopod 5.

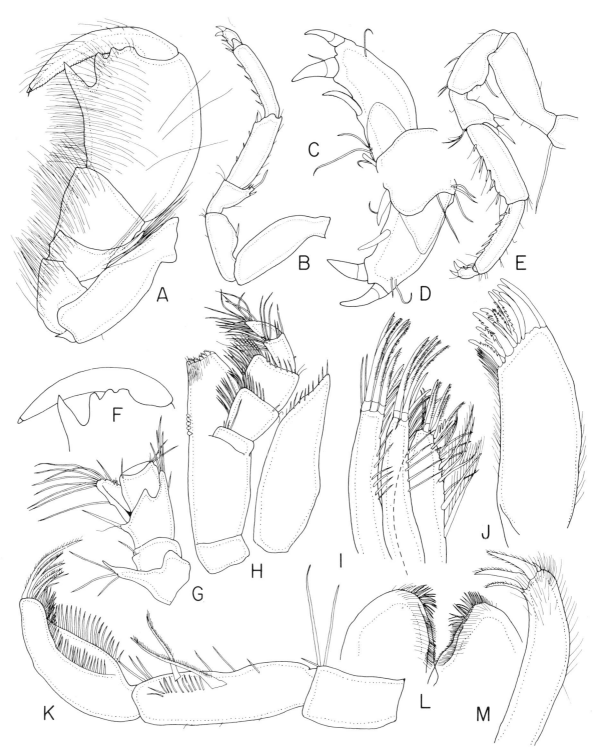

Fig. 3. Stenetrium armatum Haswell, 1881: A, male peraeopod I; B, peraeopod II; C,
dactylus of peraeopod II; D, dactylus of peraeopod VII; E, peraeopod VII; F, dactylus and palm of male peraeopod I; G, antenna 2 peduncle; H, maxilliped; I, maxilla 2;
J, maxilla 1 exopod; K, mandibular palp; L, hypopharynx; M, maxilla 1 endopod.

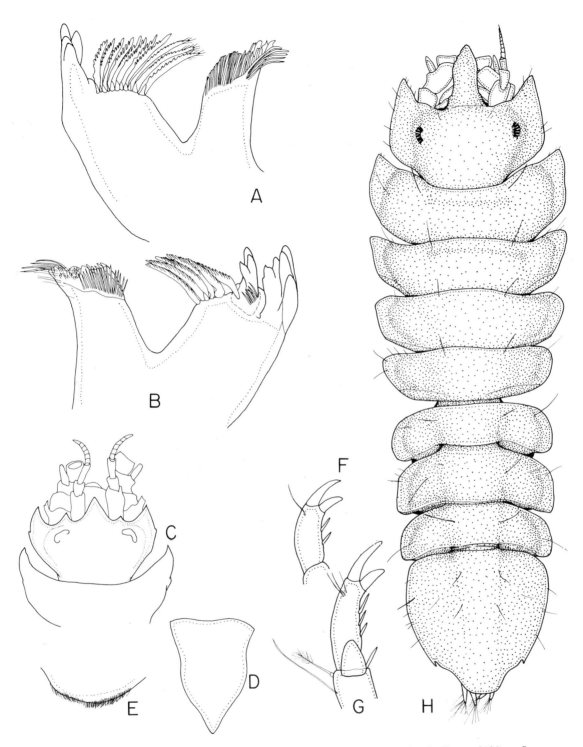

Fig. 4. <u>Stenetrium armatum</u> Haswell, 1881: A, right mandible; B, left mandible; C, detail, cephalon with pointed rostrum; D, female pleopod 2 (sympod); E, labrum. <u>Stenetrium abyssale</u> Wolff, 1962: F, dactylus of peraeopod II; G, dactylus of peraeopod VI; H, allotype female (8.6 mm long).

otelson with fused bases and two rami and with lateral outer edges parallel up to half length then rounded so as to form somewhat elliptical operculum over male pleopods 2. Male pleopods 2 with bases composing most of area of pleopod and elongated into medially pointed basal hooks. Endopod ending in tuft of long setae with lateral subapical fringe of shorter setae. Exopod with large spine on basal segment and distal segment short and lobed.

Female pleopods 2 operculate, posterior margin pointed. (Immature females have tip of operculate pleopod notched with two small lobes on distal margin, showing fusion of two bilateral pleopods.) Pleopod 3 (alike in males and females) large, operculate to branchial cavity.

Exopod of pleopod 3 with two segments divided by oblique joint. Endopod widest at about half width of exopod; six apical setae on rounded apical margin. Exopod of pleopod 4 with two segments ending in medially directed point; 11 apical and lateral marginal setae. No setae on lobe of endopod, which is about half as wide as exopod. Pleopod 5 uniramous, obtusely pointed with eight marginal setae.

Measurements. One male, 12.7 mm long; one male and one female, each 12 mm long.

Type locality. New South Wales: 'Port Jackson, among algae a few feet below the low water mark' [Haswell, 1881, p. 479]. Haswell apparently described the species from a single individual which he collected. No type specimens were actually designated by him, but in the collection of the Australian Museum the specimens examined here from Port Jackson were found (AM P3376). They probably were examined by Haswell.

Distribution. The species is distributed in southeastern Australia from at least Port Stephens, New South Wales (AM P3377), to the Gulf St. Vincent on the south coast. Several males and females in the collection of the South Australian Museum (Adelaide) were collected at the Gulf St. Vincent near Adelaide.

Remarks. The rostrum on the frontal margin of the cephalon of S. armatum is apparently variable in shape and includes both broadly rounded and produced types. The shape varies independently of sex; thus the shape of the rostrum is apparently not a sexually dimorphic character.

If one critically compares Haswell's drawings of 1881 and 1885 with the drawings of Hansen [1905, p. XIX], it is difficult to believe that the specimens redescribed here are the same species described by Haswell. Hansen based his redescription on tracings 'kindly forwarded to me a long time ago' by someone apparently associated with Haswell. There were many differences which neither Stebbing nor I could resolve, and so specimens from the Australian Museum were obtained. The specimens definitely represent the same species as described by Haswell. They were collected at Port Jackson but are not actually holotypes or allotypes.

Stenetrium abyssale Wolff
Figs. 4F-4H

Stenetrium abyssale Wolff, 1962, p. 25, figs. 1, 3-5.--Schultz, 1978, p. 249.

Diagnosis. Rostrum elongate; no well-defined frontal processes on frontal margin of cephalon.

Description. Eyes of few ocelli. Cephalon about as wide as widest part of pleotelson. Cephalon with anterolateral angles long and obtusely pointed, with only slight indications of frontal processes on frontal margin. Rostrum longer than broad, with acutely pointed tip. Antenna 1 with many more articles in flagellum of male than in that of female (21 versus 13 on two specimens).

Convex inner margins of rami of male pleopod 1 overlap. Exopod of male pleopod 1 'distinctly 1-jointed.' Two inferior dactyl claws on peraeopod II; three on dactylus of peraeopod VI. Distal dactyl claw on apex smaller than unguis. Ventral keel on VII only. Uropods very short and folded inwardly, with bases and part of both rami hidden beneath pleotelson (dorsal view).

Measurements. Holotype male, 9.9 mm long; allotype female (from a different station), 8.6 mm long.

Type locality. Galathea station 664, northeast of New Zealand, Kermadec Trench; 36°34'S, 178°57'W; February 24, 1952; 4540 m; holotype. Galathea station 602; Tasman Sea; 43°58'S, 165°25'E; January 15, 1952; 4510 m; allotype.

Affinities. Wolff [1962] compared the species to S. syzygus Barnard and S. saldanha Barnard from South Africa, but it is more correctly compared to S. acutum Vanhöffen. Stenetrium abyssale has a longer rostrum and fewer ocelli than S. acutum. The posterior margin of the pleotelson is acutely pointed or produced in specimens of S. acutum. The general body configuration of S. abyssale looks much like that of Protallocoxa weddellensis Schultz [1978], but the coxal segments on peraeonal segment I are definitely not free in S. abyssale.

Stenetrium acutum Vanhöffen
Figs. 5A-5I, 6A-6G, and 7A-7G

Stenetrium acutum Vanhöffen, 1914, p. 546, figs. 72, 73a-73h.--Nordenstam, 1933, p. 276.--Wolff, 1962, p. 24.--Kussakin, 1967, p. 300.

Diagnosis. Anterolateral projections on cephalon extremely long (two or more times length of frontal processes). Posterior margin of pleotelson with acutely pointed medial process.

Description. Eyes of about 23 ocelli. Length about one third of width; body margins parallel for almost entire length. Cephalon broadly attached to peraeonal segment I with long well-developed anterolateral angles and small obtuse frontal angles. Rostrum about as long as it is

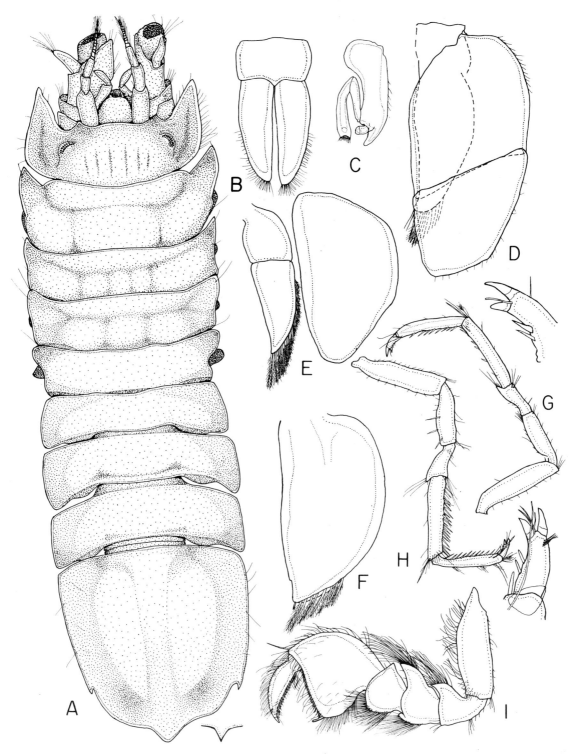

Fig. 5. Stenetrium acutum Vanhöffen, 1914: A, male (12 mm long); B-F male pleopods 1-5, respectively; G, peraeopod II with detail of dactylus (illustration shows twist at carpal-meral joint); H, peraeopod VII with detail of dactylus; I, male peraeopod I.

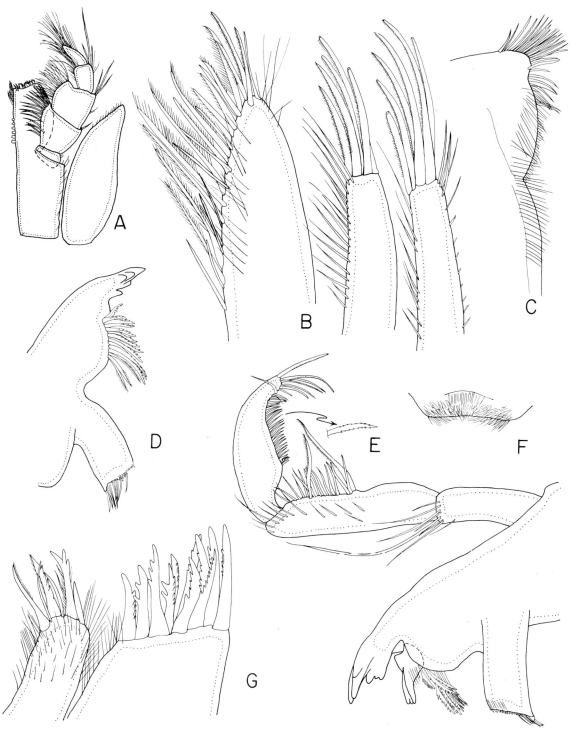

Fig. 6. Stenetrium acutum Vanhöffen, 1914: A, maxilliped; B, maxilla 2; C, hypopharynx; D, right mandible; E, left mandible; F, labrum; G, maxilla 1.

wide with obtusely pointed or broadly rounded frontal margin. Cephalon creased with longitudinally directed furrows (especially in large specimens).

Antenna 1 of female with at least seven flagellar articles; male with up to 14 flagellar articles. Antenna 2 without spine on peduncular segment 1. Antenna squama shorter than length and

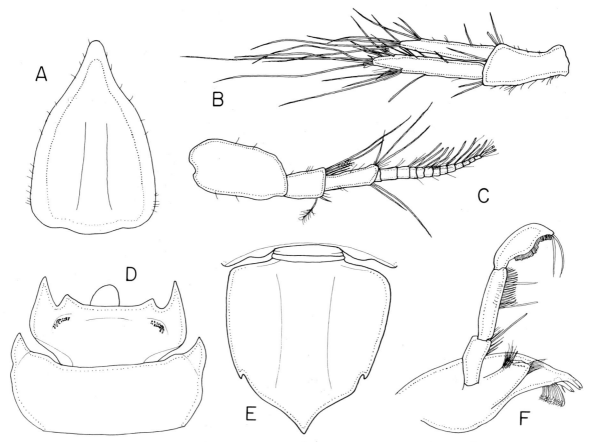

Fig. 7. Stenetrium acutum Vanhöffen, 1914: A, female pleopod 2 (sympod); B, uropod; C, antenna 1, male; D, cephalon and peraeonal segment I;, female (10.5 mm long); E, pleon, female (10.5 mm long); F, left mandible, female (10.5 mm).

width of peduncular segment 3. Manus of peraeopod I with propodus as long as it is wide, without any large teeth except one moderately long terminal tooth on palm. Dactylus as long as palm, with row of small teeth of uniform size on inner margin. Outer edges of merus and ischium moderately produced and pointed. Two claws on dactyli of peraeopods II-VII; two moderately large inferior dactyl spines on each. Uropods elongate with many long setae.

Anterolateral angles of peraeonal segments I-IV produced anteriorly, I most produced. Coxal extensions showing on segments I-IV, some obscurely (dorsal view). Segments V and VI with subquadrate lateral edges only slightly produced posteriorly. Pleotelson slightly longer than broad with smooth lateral margins ending in produced posterior border.

Measurements. Male up to 12 mm long; females up to 11 mm long.

Type locality. Gauss station; off Antarctic continent; 66°02'S, 90°20'E; December 23, 1902, and March 30, 1903; 385 m. Holotype male and allotype female. Three other males 8, 8, and 7 mm long and five females 11, 9.5, 9, 8.5, and 6 mm

long were taken in addition to the type specimens.

Distribution. The species is apparently circum-Antarctic in distribution, being recorded from many locations around the continent. The depth range is from 150 to 3397 m. One male 11 mm long and two females 10.5 and 8.5 mm long were recorded at '...Tiefe vom südlichen Eismeer' at 65°16'S and 80°28'E at 3397 m on February 25, 1902, by Vanhöffen [1914]. It was taken near Seymour Island at 150 m by the Swedish Antarctic Expedition [Nordenstam, 1933]. Kussakin [1967, p. 300] recorded a male and a female at Ob station 203 at 66°12'04"S and 57°42'02"E about February 2, 1957, at 560 m.

It is recorded here from four Eltanin and two Vema stations. Eltanin stations; sta. 6-410; Argentine Basin; start at 61°18'S, 56°09'W; 220 m; finish at 61°20'S, 56°10'W; 240 m; December 31, 1962; one female 5 mm long. Sta. 6-418; Bransfield Strait; start at 62°38.9'S, 56°10.2'W; 426 m; finish at 62°39.9'S, 56°07.8'W; 311 m January 2, 1963; one female 10.5 mm long (illustrated here). Sta. 6-430; start at 62°38'S, 59°37'W; 681 m; finish at 62°41'S, 59°23'W; 1409 m; January 7, 1963, four males 7.5-10.5 mm long; four females 5.5-11 mm long; one specimen, sex undetermined;

one 8-mm female was gravid. Sta. 12-1003; north-east of Joinville Island; start at 62°41'S, 54°43'W; 210 m; finish at 62°41'S, 54°43'W; 220 m; March 15, 1964; one gravid female 11.5 mm long; one male fragment; two fragments, sex undetermined. Vema stations: Sta. 17-99; South Atlantic, slope off Península Valdés, Argentina; 44°25'S, 59°19'W; January 19, 1961; 150-154 m; one male 7.5 mm long. Sta. 17-101; South Atlantic, slope east of Mar del Plata, Argentina; 38°13'S, 55°19'W; January 19, 1961; 450-454 m; one male 6 mm long.

Affinities. The general body shape, the spination of the dactyli of peraeopod II, and the type of manus as well as other characters, such as spination on the lacinia mobilis and minute serrations on the edges of the pleotelson, are similar to the respective structures of S. abyssale Wolff. However, the body of S. abyssale has rounded corners on the peraeonal segments, and the posterior margin of the pleotelson is not acutely produced. Also, the rostrum is longer in S. abyssale than in S. acutum.

Stenetrium bartholomei Barnard
Figs. 8A-8K and 9A-9J

Stenetrium bartholomei Barnard, 1940, p. 431, fig. 19 (right).--Wolff, 1962, p. 23.

Diagnosis. Shape of manus of male peraeopod I unique.

Description. (Barnard [1940] illustrated only male peraeopod I. A male 6 mm long and a female from Natal were used for the illustrations here.) Eyes somewhat reniform. Anterolateral angles of cephalon acute, frontal processes sharply pointed. Rostrum triangular, frontal margin round, width at base equals length. Antenna 1 with second peduncular segment shortest, one-half length of segment 1; segment 3 two-thirds length of segment 1. Ventral keels prominent on all peraeonal segments. Basis of pleopod 2 of male terminates in acute point; exopod with elongate curved tip; endopod with produced, pointed apex.

Palm of manus of male peraeopod I with irregular bladelike teeth; dactylus broad, only slightly longer than palm, with very small, short terminal claw. Female with propodus longer than broad, with large terminal spine on palm of manus thus formed; length of flattened dactylus with terminal claw about as long as that of palm.

Measurements. Male, 7 mm long; female, 6.5 mm long.

Type locality. Still Bay, South Africa, littoral.

Distribution. Cape Peninsula to Natal shores at Mbotyi, littoral. Additional specimens, one male 6 mm long and one female 5 mm long with oostegites (UCT CP 423U), were taken at the shore of the Cape Peninsula. At Port Elizabeth one male, one gravid female, and nine juveniles were collected in 1932

and one male and one female in 1936. At the Natal shores at Mbotyi, three males 2.5-7 mm long, one female 4.5 mm long, and one specimen (sex undetermined) 7 mm long (UCT NA-191K) were taken.

Affinities. Barnard [1940] compared this species to S. diazi Barnard [1920].

Stenetrium beddardi Kussakin
Figs. 10A-10K and 11A-11J

Stenetrium beddardi Kussakin, 1967, p. 303, figs. 50-52.

Diagnosis. Shape of male pleopod 2 most probably diagnostic.

Description. (This redescription is based on specimens from Eltanin station 9-740.) Eyes of about 18 ocelli. Cephalon with rounded lateral edges ending in acutely pointed anterolateral processes. Frontal processes shorter than anterolateral processes. Antenna 1 with 13-17 flagellar articles. Peraeonal segment I with acute anterolateral points; segment III with least acute points; IV with notch in lateral border above coxal processes. Coxal processes show (dorsal view) on lateral margins of I-IV. Peraeopod I of male (and female) with large setae in row on palm and only one palmar tooth. Palm with one large seta. Pleotelson with subparallel margins, distinct posterolateral notches, and rounded posterior margin. Basis of male pleopod 2 with distal margin only slightly produced; exopod well defined; apex of endopod strongly produced. (This male, 7 mm long, had just molted the posterior half of its integument.)

Measurements. Holotype male, 7.55 mm long; allotype gravid female, 9.55 mm long.

Type locality. Ob station 479; about 1000 km northeast of the Falkland Islands; 45°16'S, 54°54'W; June 15, 1958; 680 m.

Distribution. Two females, one gravid, at nearby Ob station 480; 43°41'S, 59°34'W; June 16, 1958; 399-500 m. Eltanin station 9-740; Drake Passage, south of Cape Horn; start at 56°06.2'S, 66°19'W; 494 m; finish at 56°06.5'S, 66°30'W; 384 m; September 18, 1963; 23 males 3-7.5 mm long; 27 females 3-8 mm long; and 6 males and 5 female fragments; 13 fragments, sex undetermined.

Affinities. Kussakin [1967] compared the ischium and carpus of peraeopod I of S. beddardi to those structures of S. haswelli Beddard [1886]. It is also somewhat like S. diazi Barnard and S. saldanha Barnard. All three have similar body configurations, cephalons, peraeonal segments I-IV, and pleotelsons. However, the somewhat triangular rostrum, the pleotelson, which is longer than wide, and the very long pointed male pleopod 2 set S. beddardi apart from other species. The species is also much like S. acutum Vanhöffen, but the male pleopod 2 is different.

Remarks. See remarks section under S. dentimanum Kussakin.

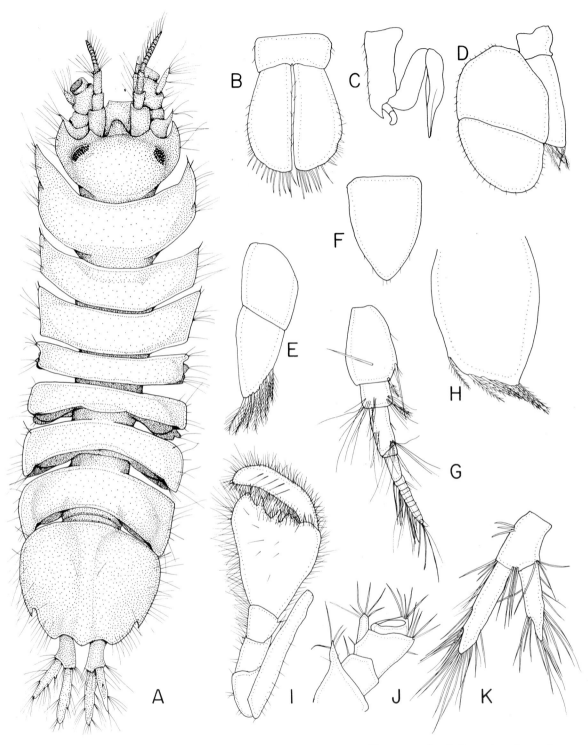

Fig. 8. _Stenetrium bartholomei_ Barnard, 1940: A, male (6 mm long); B-D, male pleopods
1-3, respectively; E, exopod of pleopod 4; F, female pleopod 2 (sympod); G, antenna 1;
H, pleopod 5; I, male peraeopod I; J, antenna 1 peduncle; K, uropod.

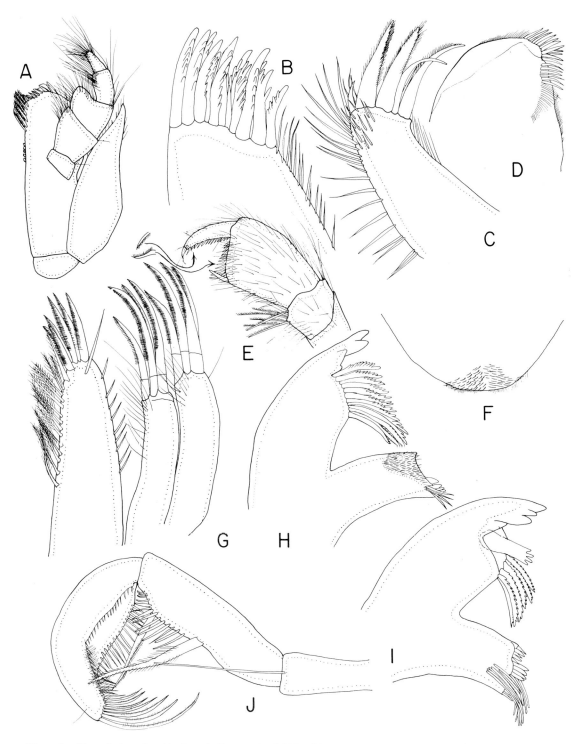

Fig. 9. *Stenetrium bartholomei* Barnard, 1940: A, maxilliped; B, maxilla 1 exopod; C, maxilla 1 endopod; D, hypopharynx; E, female peraeopod I; F, labrum; G, maxilla 2; H, right mandible; I, left mandible; J, mandibular palp.

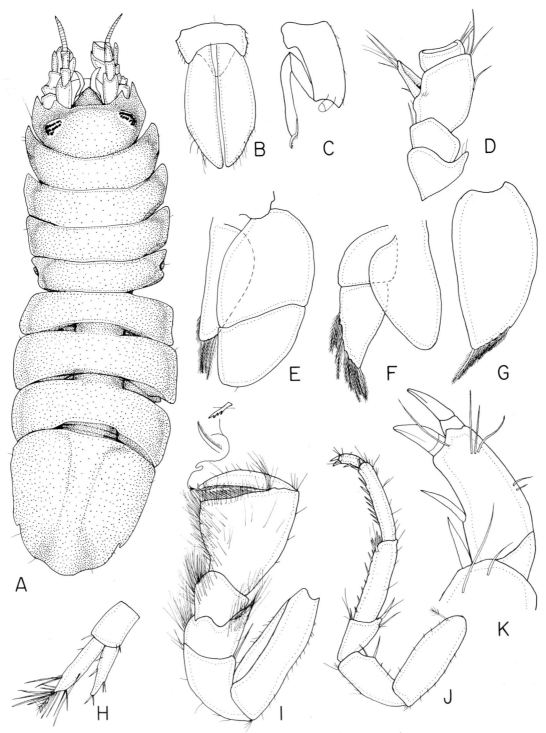

Fig. 10. _Stenetrium beddardi_ Kussakin, 1967: A, male (7 mm long); B and C, male pleopods 1 and 2, respectively; D, antenna 2 peduncle; E-G, pleopods 3-5, respectively; H, uropod; I, male peraeopod I; J, peraeopod III; K, dactylus of peraeopod III.

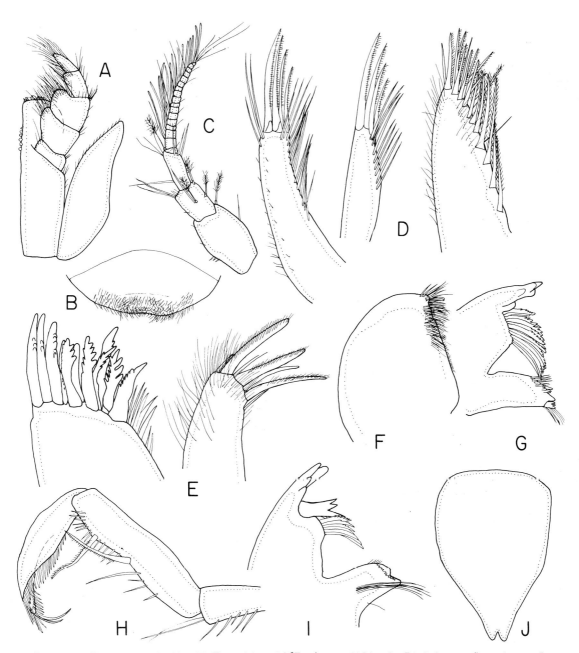

Fig. 11. <u>Stenetrium</u> <u>beddardi</u> Kussakin, 1967: A, maxilliped; B, labrum; C, antenna 1;
D, maxilla 2; E, maxilla 1; F, hypopharynx; G, right mandible; H, mandibular palp; I,
left mandible; J, female pleopod 2 (sympod).

<u>Senetrium</u> <u>crassimanum</u> Barnard

<u>Senetrium</u> <u>crassimanum</u> Barnard, 1914, p. 217, pl.
  20A; 1920, p. 404.--Wolff, 1962, p. 23.--
  Kensley, 1975, p. 40; 1976, p. 320.

  <u>Diagnosis</u>. Body covered with hairlike setae.
Shape of manus of male peraeopod I unique.
  <u>Description</u>. Body covered with hairlike setae.
Eyes reniform. Anterolateral angles of cephalon
acutely pointed; frontal processes not well
developed. Rostrum longer than broad with blunt
apex. Antenna 1 with flagellum of 12 articles.
Antenna 2 shorter than length of body. Male peraeopod I with manus about as broad as it is long
with three pointed teeth on palm; dactylus narrow,
extending to carpus beyond palm. Female with
elongate propodus with short palm; propodus not
much broader than other segments of peraeopod.
  <u>Measurements</u>. Male, 7 mm long.

Type locality. St. James, False Bay, South Africa, under rocks at low tide; April 29, 1912. Male and gravid female.

Distribution. False Bay to Still Bay [Kensley, 1975], South Africa. It was also recorded by Barnard [1914] during the Pieter Faure cruises. Kensley [1976] recorded the species from Île Saint-Paul and Île Amsterdam.

Affinities. Barnard's description contained very little information for distinguishing this species from others of the genus save the illustration of male peraeopod I. No large coxal projection is present on the lateral margins of peraeonal segment I; indeed even segment IV is shown with a smooth edge [Barnard, 1914, pl. 20A]. The lack of coxal processes (dorsal view) is also characteristic of another species from South Africa, to be described here later. It, however, is not otherwise much like that new species. Male pleopod 2 and female peraeopod I are much like those of S. bartholomei Barnard [1940].

Remarks. The specimens from Île Saint-Paul and Île Amsterdam were not illustrated or described by Kensley [1976].

Stenetrium dagama Barnard

Stenetrium dagama Barnard, 1920, p. 399, pl. 16, figs. 28, 29.--Wolff, 1962, p. 24.--Kensley, 1975, p. 40.

Diagnosis. Shape of manus of male peraeopod I unique.

Description. Eyes narrow, oblong, and curved. Anterolateral corners acutely pointed--frontal processes? Rostrum broader than long. Antenna 1 with flagellum of about 15 articles. Male peraeopod I with triangular manus; palm straight, with many small setae and one large spine; dactylus about as long as palm. Female peraeopod I similar but smaller than that of male. Distal margin of pleotelson obscurely trilobed.

Measurements. Male, 7.5 mm long.

Type locality. Thirty kilometers off Cape Point, South Africa; 420 m; in hexactinellid sponge. Four males, six gravid females.

Distribution. Off Cape Point region. Two males were also taken at 93 km south and east of Table Mountain not far from the type locality at 347 m among siliceous sponges. Kensley [1975] added a record from nearby Still Bay.

Affinities. Wolff [1962] distinguished this species from others by the structure of the ventral keels and the configuration of male peraeopod I.

Stenetrium dalmeida Barnard

Stenetrium dalmeida Barnard, 1920, p. 400.--Wolff, 1962, p. 24.

Diagnosis. Not possible; the species was never illustrated.

Description. Eyes narrow, oblong, and curved. Anterolateral angles acutely pointed on cephalon. Rostrum broader than long. Antenna 1 with flagellum of 12 articles. Male peraeopod I with palm 'a little oblique with one strong acute tooth in the centre and another near the hinge (both teeth lacking in the smaller male, 5 mm long), one small spine on the defining angle, finger matching palm...' [Barnard, 1920, p. 400].

Measurements. Male, 7.5 mm long.

Type locality. Eighty kilometers off Cape Peninsula; 420 m. Two males.

Distribution. Off Cape Peninsula, South Africa. A female was found 29 km northeast of Cape point at 246 m.

Affinities. Barnard [1920] distinguished the species from S. dagama Barnard by the acute but not strongly produced outer angle of antenna 1. Also, differences in the ventral keel, peraeopod I, and pattern of setation are present.

Stenetrium dentimanum Kussakin

Stenetrium dentimanum Kussakin, 1967, p. 300, figs. 47-49.

Diagnosis. Configuration of manus of male peraeopod I with teeth mostly near hinge side of palm.

Description. Eyes large. Anterolateral corners of cephalon elongate and acutely pointed. Frontal processes well defined and shorter than anterolateral processes. Rostrum elongate and broadly rounded apically. Antenna 1 with about 23 flagellar articles. Coxal processes visible (dorsal view) on peraeonal segments III-IV. Peraeopod I of male with large teeth on palm. Posterolateral notches of pleotelson well defined; posterior border produced. Basis of male pleopod 2 with produced distal margin projecting to about length of exopod (?); apex of endopod blunt.

Measurements. Holotype male, 9 mm long; one female (Ob station 480), 11.6 mm long.

Type locality. Ob station 479; about 1000 km northeast of the Falkland Islands; 45°16'S, 59°54'W; June 15, 1958; 680 m.

Distribution. A female 11.6 mm long was taken at nearby Ob station 480 at 43°41'S and 59°54'W on June 16, 1958, at 399-500 m.

Affinities. Kussakin [1967] made no comparisons with any other species. The configuration of the manus of the male peraeopod I and the 23 flagellar articles on the flagellum of antenna 1 set the species apart from S. acutum Vanhöffen and S. beddardi Kussakin.

Remarks. Both S. beddardi Kussakin and S. dentimanum were collected at Ob stations 479 and 480. Stenetrium dentimanum is based on a male and a female from each station; S. beddardi is based on a male and three females from station 479 and another female from station 480. For both species the type locality is Ob station 479.

Stenetrium diazi Barnard
Figs. 12A-12L and 13A-13H

Stenetrium diazi Barnard, 1920, p. 401, pl. 16,
    figs. 30-32.--Wolff, 1062, p. 23.

Diagnosis. Manus of peraropod I elongate with
three broad teeth on palm. Shape of male pleopod
I unique.

Description. (A male 5.2 mm long from near the
type locality is illustrated here.) Cephalon with
acutely pointed anterolateral processes and shorter, rounded frontal processes. Eyes large, of
about 22 ocelli. Peraeopod segment I with acutely
pointed anterolateral processes and coxal grooves
on lateral margin; dorsal view of segment II with
indications of coxal processes; segment III with
coxal processes conspicuous; segment IV with coxal
processes large and with produced anterolateral
margins. Segment V with subquadrate edges and VII
with acute posterolateral edges. Coxal processes
show in dorsal view on posterior margin of segments V-VII. Pleotelson with large posterolateral
notches; posterior margin produced and broadly
rounded.

Propodus of peraeopod I with width about two-
thirds length and with three large bladelike
extensions on palm. Dactylus longer than palm,
ending in long unguis. Male pleopods I wider
nearer apex than at base near sympod; apex formed
by both rami triangular. Five comblike long setae
on outer and middle rami of maxilla 2.

Measurements. Male, 6 mm long; female, 5 mm
long.

Type locality. Buffel's Bay (in False Bay),
South Africa. Two males, three females (one gravid), and four juveniles. A third male, 5.2 mm
long, was also taken in False Bay (UCT FAL 282A).

Affinities. The species is related to S. crassimanum Barnard according to him, but the propodus
is much longer than it is wide, and the palm of
peraeopod is differently shaped in S. diazi.

Stenetrium fractum Chilton

Stenetrium fractum Chilton, 1884, p. 249, pl. 18,
    figs. 3a-3f.--Hansen, 1905, p. 319.--Nierstrasz,
    1941, p. 281.--Hurley, 1961, p. 261.--Wolff,
    1962, p. 22.

Diagnosis. Lateral margins of pleotleson 'irregularly serrate.'

Description. (The sex of the 'much crushed'
type specimen is probably female and was not determined with confidence according to Chilton.
Its cephalon was not described or illustrated.)
Antenna 1 with five 'segments' in flagellum. Antenna 2 as long as body. Peraeopod I with 'palm
transverse, defined by a stout tooth, and armed
with strong serrated setae.' Dactylus narrow and
pointed, about as long as palm. Lateral margin of
pleotelson irregularly serrate, ending in rounded
produced posterior margin [Chilton, 1884, pl. 17,
fig. 3f].

Measurements. Holotype (sex undetermined, but
probably female), 4.2 mm long.

Type locality. Lyttleton Harbour, New Zealand,
shallow water.

Affinities. The poorly described species was
compared only with the generic definition of Haswell [1881]. Nierstrasz [1941] and Hurley [1961]
simply included the species in a list. It and S.
glauerti Nicholls have different ornamentation on
the lateral borders on the margins of the pleotelson, but the serrations are irregular in shape and
size on S. fractum Chilton and regularly serrate
or sawtoothlike on S. glauerti.

Remarks. The validity of the specimen as a distinct species is still to be determined morpholo-
gically; however, it is geographically so far away
from other species that it is highly probable that
it is a distinct species.

Stenetrium glauerti Nicholls
Fig. 14

Stenetrium glauerti Nicholls, 1929, p. 373, figs.
    15-22.--Wolff, 1962, p. 23.

Diagnosis. Configuration of male peraeopod I
unique.

Description. (A female marked cotype (AM P9248)
forms the basis of the following redescription.)
Eyes of about 12 ocelli. Cephalon about as wide
as peraeonal segment I. Cephalon with anterolateral and frontal angles acutely pointed. Rostrum
large, longer than broad, rounded apically. Slight
indications of coxal process on segments I-IV
(dorsal view). Segment V shortest with coxal
processes on posterior border. Segments VI and
VII with smooth lateral borders, coxal processes
show prominently on VI only. Pleotelson as broad
as segment I with regularly serrate (sawtoothlike)
lateral margins. Posterolateral notches prominent
and posterior margin broadly rounded and slightly
produced on pleotelson.

Measurements. Male, 5 mm long; gravid female
slightly smaller.

Type locality. Bathurst Point, Rottnest Island,
western Australia. Four males, seven females (six
gravid), and three juveniles; September, 1928.

Affinities. See affinities section under Stenetrium fractum Chilton.

Remarks. The illustration of the cephalon by
Nicholls [1929] seems to contain eyes with more
than a 'few (6-7) ocelli.' The female marked cotype (4.4 mm long) at the Australian Museum,
Sydney, has at least 12 ocelli.

Stenetrium haswelli Beddard

Stenetrium haswelli Beddard, 1886a, p. 103; 1886b,
    p. 9, pl. 4, figs. 1-8.--Hansen, 1905, p. 321.--
    Kussakin, 1967, p. 306.

Diagnosis. Dorsal view of coxal extensions on
peraeonal segments I-IV unique.

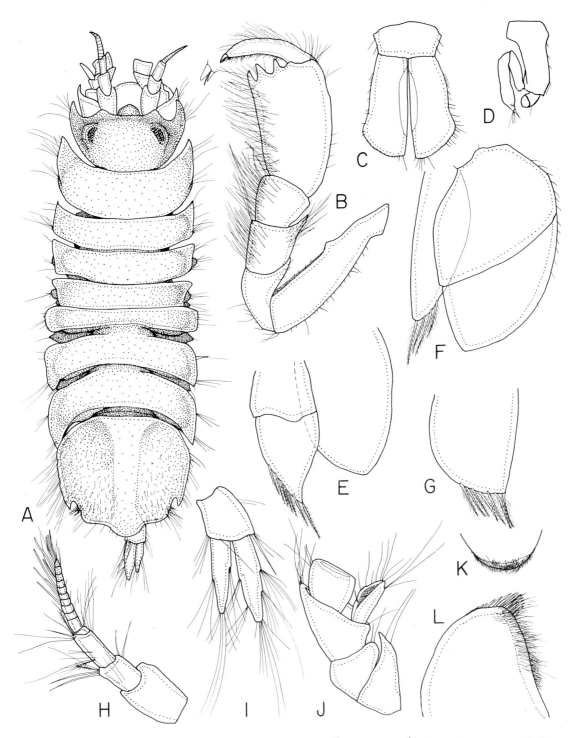

Fig. 12. Stenetrium diazi Barnard, 1920: A, male (5.2 mm long); B, male peraeopod I; C-G, male pleopods 1-5, respectively; H, antenna 1; I, uropod; J, antenna 2 peduncle; K, labrum; ;L, hypopharynx.

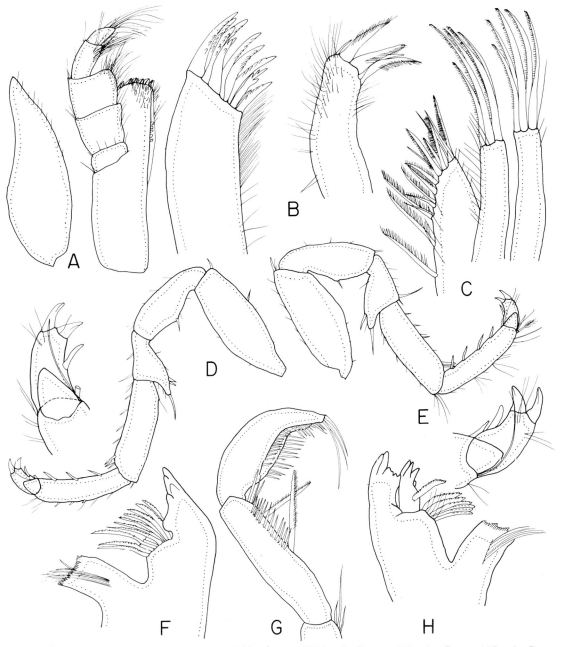

Fig. 13. _Stenetrium diazi_ Barnard, 1920: A, maxilliped; B, maxilla 1; C, maxilla 2; D, peraeopod II with detail of dactylus; E, peraeopod VII with detail of dactylus; F, right mandible; G, mandibular palp; H, left mandible.

Description. Eyes present. Anterolateral edges of cephalon pointed; frontal processes present. Rostrum apparently long and truncate [Beddard, 1886b, pl. 4, fig. 1]. Edges of peraeonal segments II-IV indented, with coxal processes projecting from below showing in indentations. Coxal processes project from posterolateral or posterior margins of segments V-VII. Peraeopod I with ovate manus; palm straight without prominent teeth; dactylus narrow and pointed. No posterolateral notch on margin of pleotelson (at least not in Beddard's illustration). Posterior margin of pleotelson rounded and slightly produced.

Measurements. Male, 16 mm long.

Type locality. _Challenger_ station 320; Argentine Basin, off Río de la Plata; 37°17'S, 53°52'W; February 1876; 1097 m.

Affinities. Beddard compared the species to _S._

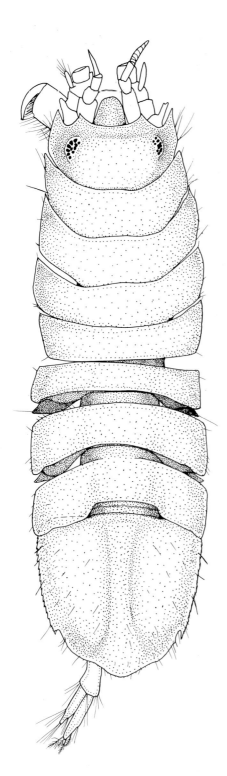

Fig. 14. Stenetrium glauerti Nicholls, 1929: Female (4.4 mm long).

armatum Haswell and S. chiltoni Stebbing. Kussa-kin [1967, p. 306] stated that his species S. bed-dardi might be S. haswelli, but he did not make any extended arguments to prove it. The species differ most obviously in the shape of the pleotel-son and male peraeopod I. Also, the edges of per-aeonal segments II-IV are indented in S. haswelli but not in S. beddardi (Figure 8A).

Remarks. The lack of posterolateral notches in the margins of the pleotelson in S. haswelli is perhaps an error in Beddard's illustration.

Stenetrium macrochirum Nicholls

Stenetrium macrochirum Nicholls, 1929, p. 363, figs. 1-10.--Wolff, 1962, p. 23.

Diagnosis. Shape of manus of male peraeopod I unique.

Description. Eyes reniform. Frontal margin of cephalon with short, but acutely pointed, antero-lateral margins; frontal processes short, but pointed. Rostrum short, triangular, and with rounded apex. Antenna 1 with five articles (fe-male) or 12 articles (male). Antenna 2 about as long as body. Male peraeopod I with manus longer than broad with three spines on palm; dactylus wide, about as long as palm. Female peraeopod I with manus longer than wide, only slightly wider than other peraeopodal segments; palm with long spine on edge and dactylus only slightly longer than palm. Posterolateral notches well developed on pleotelson; posterior margin of pleotelson rounded and slightly produced.

Measurements. Male and gravid female, each 5.9 mm long.

Type locality. Dongarra, western Australia, on seaweed. Three males, six (three gravid) females, two juveniles, one 'larva'; April 1928.

Affinities. It is not compared to any other species by Nicholls.

Stenetrium rotundatum Vanhöffen

Stenetrium rotundatum Vanhöffen, 1914, p. 548, figs. 74a-74c.--Wolff, 1962, p. 24.

Diagnosis. Structure of male pleopod 2 unique.
Description. (Vanhöffen [1914] illustrated only structures which he compared to those of his other species from Antarctica, S. acutum.) Posterior margin of pleotelson broadly rounded. Apex of sympod of male pleopod 2 not produced into lobe; two long setae extend from exopod of male pleopod 2.

Measurements. Six males and five females, each 8.5 mm long; two juveniles, 3 mm long.

Type locality. Gauss Station; April 1902 to February 1903. The location is not exactly re-corded, but it must be near the type locality of S. acutum Vanhöffen at 66°02'S, 90°20'E at 385 m.

Affinities. It is difficult to compare S. rotundatum to any other species in the genus because it was only partly described and illustrated. The broadly rounded posterior margin of the pleotelson, plus the structure of male pleopod 2, set the species apart from others in the genus from Antarctic waters.

Remarks. Although Wolff [1962] in his key to species of Stenetrium stated that the endopod of male pleopod 2 is apparently without a large mass of apical setae, it probably is not 'notched' either. If the endopod which Vanhöffen [1914, p. 548, fig. 74b] illustrated were magnified and drawn in other than line drawing, it would most probably show a spine with many very short setae surrounded by a sheath, not the notch as Wolff stated.

Stenetrium saldanha Barnard
Figs. 15A-15L, 16A-16K, 17A and 17B

Stenetrium saldanha Barnard, 1920, p. 403, pl. 16, figs. 33, 34.--Wolff, 1962, p. 24.--Kensley, 1976, p. 320.

Diagnosis. Rostrum acutely pointed and longer than acutely pointed anterolateral processes; irregular processes on margin between posterolateral notches and posterior border of pleotelson.

Description. (The description and illustrations here are of a male 6.5 mm long from the Robberg-Cape Seal region (UCT RR4E).) Eyes large, about 20 ocelli of irregular sizes. Cephalon markedly narrower than peraeon with acutely pointed rostrum, frontal and anterolateral processes. Peraeonal segments I and II with acutely pointed anterolateral angles; large coxae on lateral edges of I and barely indicated ones on II (dorsal view). Coxae of peraeopod IV visible on lateral margins. Segment V very short with lateral edges subquadrate. Pleotelson shorter than wide with minutely serrate lateral edges and irregularly serrate edges beyond posterolateral notch; posterior margin rounded and slightly produced.

Manus of peraeopod I with propodus longer than wide and with large terminal spine on palm. Dactylus about as long as palm, ending in large unguis. Single denticle on middle of palm of peraeopod (in both sexes).

Measurements. Male, 6 mm long; female, 5 mm long.

Type locality. Off South Africa, 115 km north and east of Cape St. Blaize; 228 m; male and female.

Distribution. Saldanha Bay to Cape Seal. Île Saint-Paul and Île Amsterdam [Kensley, 1976]. Saldanha Bay (UCT SB 160K). One female 30 km northeast of Cape Point at 246 m. Still Bay (UCT S54H1), fragment. Robberg-Cape Seal region; 34°S, 23°E; littoral; 11 specimens (UCT RR 4E); largest female 7 mm long; smallest, damaged specimen (sex undetermined) 3 mm long; 6.5 mm long male illustrated here. Vema station 14-74; off Cape Town, South Africa; 34°05.5'S, 18°06'E; April 6, 1958; 179 m; male and female.

Affinities. The species is close to S. diazi Barnard in general body shape, but it differs in that the rostrum and pleopods 1 and 2 are more pointed, maxilla 2 has only four comblike setae on the outer and middle rami, and segment 3 of the mandibular palp has two rows of setae.

Remarks. The species from Île Saint-Paul and Île Amsterdam were not illustrated or described by Kensley [1976].

Stenetrium spinirostrum Nicholls
Fig. 17C

Stenetrium spinirostrum Nicholls, 1929, p. 369, figs. 23-25.--Wolff, 1962, p. 23.

Diagnosis. Shape of cephalon, shape of manus of male peraeopod I, and produced posterior border of pleotelson in combination unique.

Description. (A male marked cotype forms the basis of the following redescription (AM P9249).) Eyes of 20 to 24 ocelli. Frontal margin of cephalon with acutely pointed frontal and anterolateral projections. Anterolateral projections with tips slightly pointed inwardly. Posterolateral borders of cephalon tapered to narrow attachment to peraeonal segment I. Antenna 1 with about 12 flagellar articles. Peraeonal segment I with acutely pointed anterolateral angles and large conspicuous coxal grooves. Lateral borders of segments II and III subquadrate without conspicuous coxal processes. Coxal processes show on segment IV. Coxal processes present on posterior borders of segments V-VII. Pleotelson slightly wider than long with large posterolateral notches; posterior margin with evenly rounded medially produced margin. Uropods longer than half length of pleotelson. Male peraeopod I with large dactylus without any toothlike spines, and palm of propodus with five large bladelike teeth.

Measurements. Male and gravid female, each 7 mm long; male specimen (marked cotype) illustrated here, 5.8 mm long.

Type locality. Bathurst Point, Rottnest Island, western Australia; under stones and in fragments from the reef; September 1927 and 1928; 20 specimens.

Affinities. Nicholls [1929] compared the species to S. macrochirum Nicholls, from which it differs in the pattern of pigment distribution.

Remarks. The male illustrated here does not have the scales on the border of the rostrum, nor does it have the 17 flagellar articles on antenna 1 as described for the type specimen by Nicholls.

Stenetrium truncatum Nicholls

Stenetrium truncatum Nicholls, 1929, p. 371, figs. 11-14.--Wolff, 1962, p. 23.

Diagnosis. Anterolateral corners of cephalon shorter than or about equal to frontal corners. Pleotelson with small posterolateral notches and with broadly rounded posterior margin.

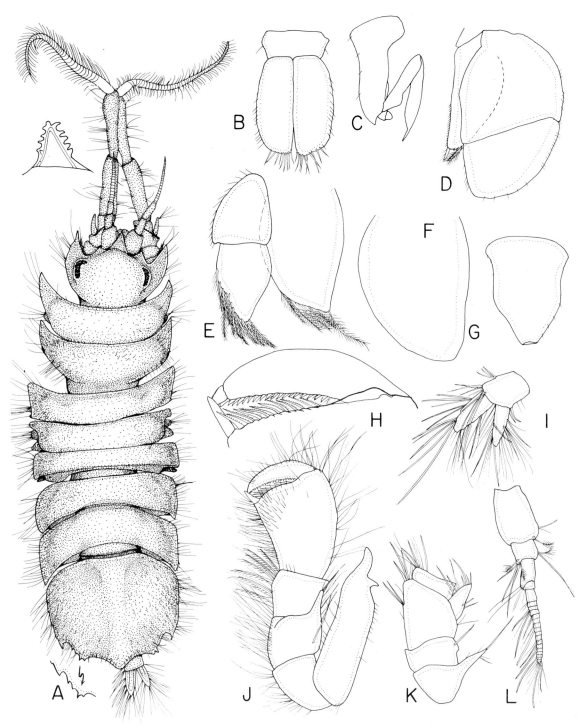

Fig. 15. _Stenetrium saldanha_ Barnard, 1920: A, male (6.5 mm long); B-F, male pleopods 1-5, respectively; female pleopod 2 (sympod); H, detail, palm of manus and
dactylus of male peraeopod I; I, uropod; J, male peraeopod I; K, antenna 2 peduncle;
L, antenna 1.

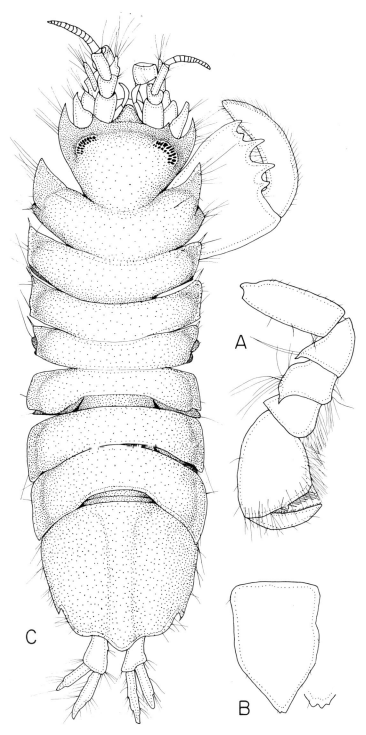

Fig. 16. *Stenetrium saldanha* Barnard, 1920: A, peraeopod II; B, antenna 2; C, maxilla 2; D, maxilla 1 exopod; E, detail, dactylus of peraeopod II; F, maxilliped; G, left mandible; H, labrum; I, maxilla 1 endopod; J, mandibular palp; K, right mandible.

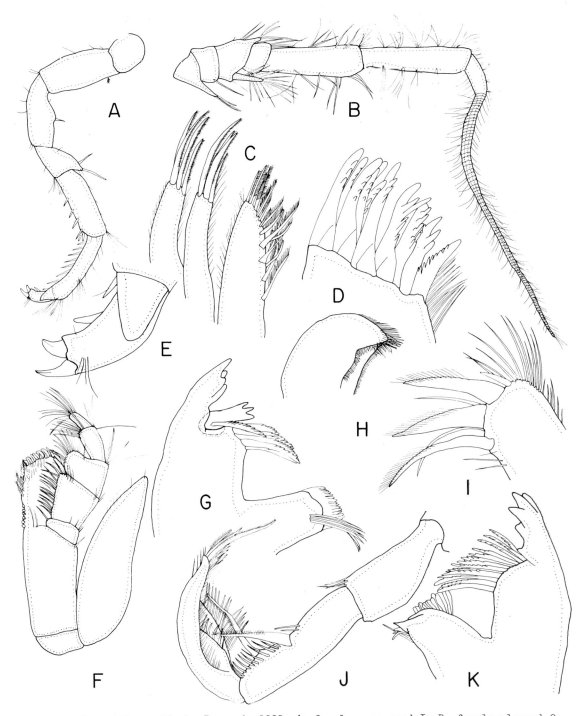

Fig. 17. Stenetrium saldanha Barnard, 1920: A, female peraeopod I; B, female pleopod 2 (sympod). Stenetrium spinirostrum Nicholls, 1929: C, male (5.8 mm long).

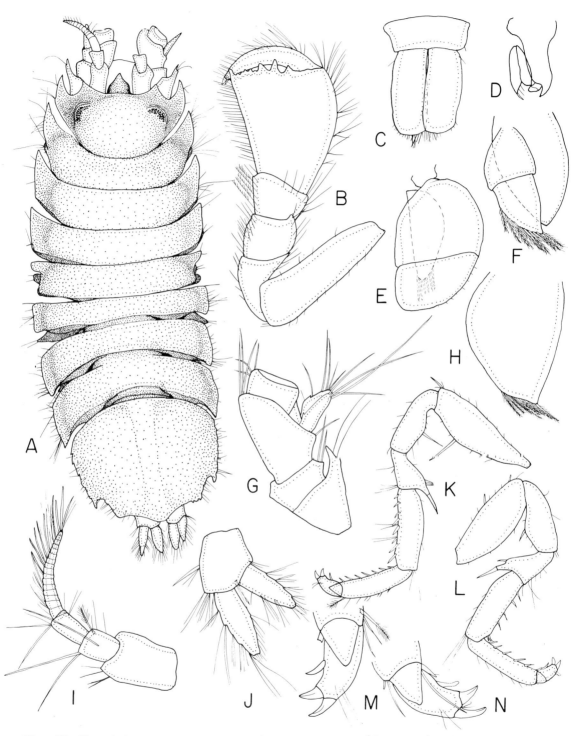

Fig. 18. _Stenetrium_ _esquartum_ n. sp.: A, holotype male (6 mm long); B, peraeopod I;
C-F, male pleopods 1-4, respectively; G, antenna 2 peduncle; H, pleopod 5; I, antenna
1; J. uropod; K, peraeopod II; L, peraeopod VII; M, dactylus of peraeopod II; N,
dactylus of peraeopod VII.

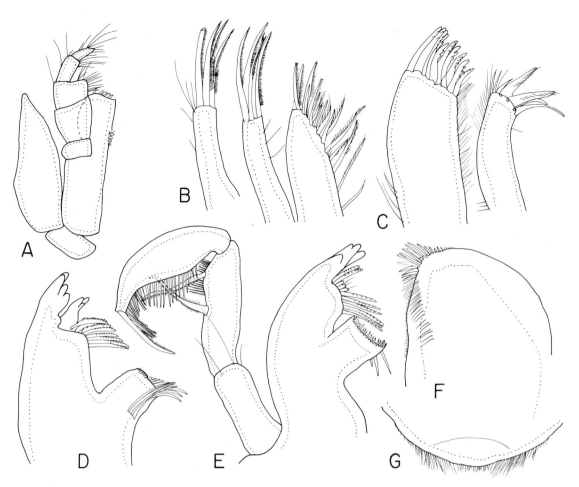

Fig. 19. *Stenetrium esquartum* n. sp.: A, maxilliped; B, maxilla 2; C, maxilla 1; D, left mandible; E, right mandible; F, hypopharynx; G, labrum.

Description. Eyes of about 18 ocelli. Frontal margin of cephalon with anterolateral and frontal processes subequal in length. Antenna 1 with about 10 flagellar articles. Antenna 2 probably shorter than length of body. Body margins subparallel. Pleotelson with small posterolateral notches and broadly rounded posterior margin. Uropods more than half length of pleotelson.

Measurements. One specimen, 5.5 mm long, sex undetermined.

Type locality. Bathurst Point, Rottnest Island, western Australia; under stones below tide mark; September 1927.

Affinities. *Stenetrium entale* Nordenstam [1946] and *S. truncatum* are the only species of *Stenetrium* in which pleopod 5 has two segments.

Remarks. Nicholls made comparisons with many other specimens, but he described *S. truncatum* from a 'single specimen, sadly mutilated' that was 5.5 mm long and whose sex was undetermined. He further stated that because it was taken after 'very heavy weather' it might be 'a stray from deeper water.' It was 'nevertheless, very readily distinguished from both the two other Western Australian forms.'

Stenetrium esquartum n. sp.
Figs. 18A-18N and 19A-19G

Diagnosis. Shape of manus of male peraeopod I unique.

Description. Eyes of about 26 ocelli. Width of body one-third length. Frontal and anterolateral processes subequal in length, both acutely pointed. Rostrum longer than broad, tapering to acute point. Peraeonal segments I-III with sharply pointed anterolateral processes. Coxal processes show on lateral edges of segments I and V (obscurely so only on III). Lateral edges of V with lateral edges square, coxal processes project from posterior margin. Pleotelson wider than long with serrate lateral margins and large posterolateral notches. Posterior margin between posterolateral notch and uropodal indentation with irregular short processes on edge. Uropods short and stout; endopod, exopod, and basis subequal in length. Antenna 2 with pointed lateral processes on peduncular segment I. Male pleopod 1 rectangular (more or less truncate), slightly longer than width of sympod.

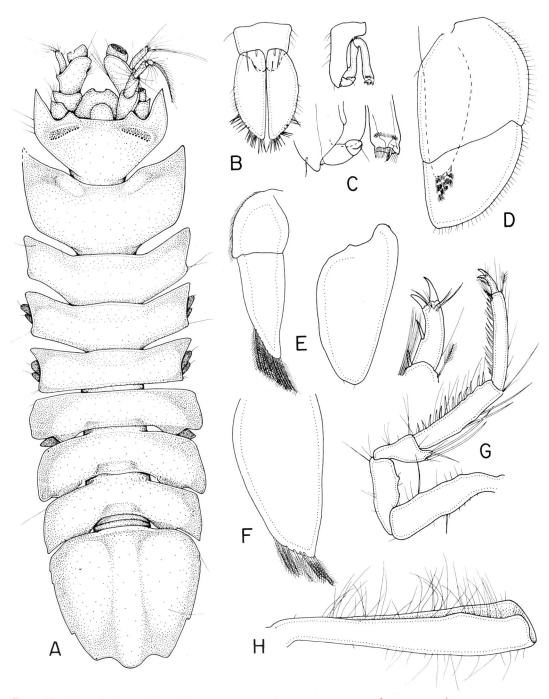

Fig. 20. *Stenetrium inflectofrons* n. sp.: A, holotype male (11 mm long); B, male pleopods 1; C, male pleopod 2 (two views); D-F, pleopods 3-5,, respectively; G, peraeopod II with detail of dactylus; H, basis of male peraeopod I (same scale as G).

Measurements. Holotype male, 5 mm long; allotype female, 5.5 mm long; paratype male, 4 mm long; five paratype females, from 3 to 5.5 mm long.

Derivation of name. 'Esquartum' is a Latinized word of no formal meaning and refers to the generally square shape of pleopods 1.

Type locality. False Bay, South Africa; 6 m deep on rocky substrate (UCT FAL 172V).

Distribution. False Bay to Qolora, South Africa. Qolora (UCT QQ 4W); one male.

Affinities. The species is much like S. saldanha Barnard, also from South Africa. The new species

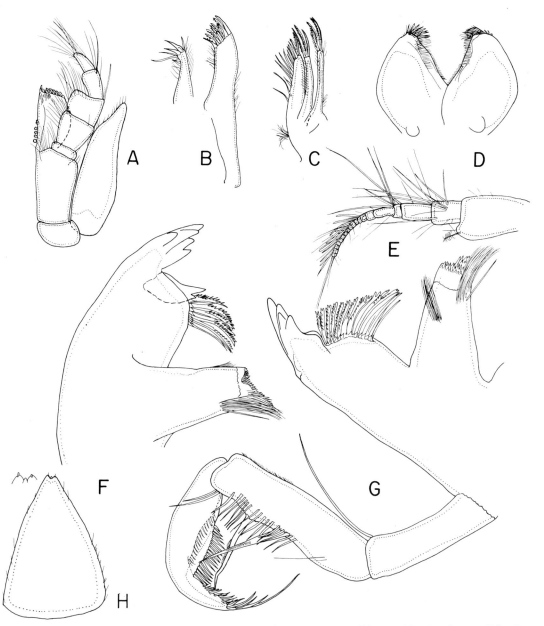

Fig. 21. <u>Stenetrium</u> <u>inflectofrons</u> n. sp.: A, maxilliped; B, maxilla 1; C, maxilla 2;
D, hypopharynx; E, antenna 1; F, left mandible; G, right mandible; H, female pleopod 2
(sympod), 8.5-mm-long specimen.

has a broader propodus on male peraeopod I; more
spines on the inner edge of the propodus of both
peraeopods II and VII; a single row of spines on
article 3 of the mandibular palp; and a more
irregular border on the edge of the pleotelson.

<u>Stenetrium</u> <u>inflectofrons</u> n. sp.
Figs. 20A-20H, 21A-21H and 22A-22F

Diagnosis. Shape of cephalon including narrow
neck and large eyes unique.

Description. Eyes elongate, wedge shaped,
tapering toward body midline, and with about 67
ocelli each. Anterolateral processes of cephalon
narrow, elongate, and acutely pointed; frontal
processes short, obtuse. Rostrum about as long as
broad, evenly rounded anteriorly, and set into
apparent excavation of frontal margin. Cephalon
noticeably narrower than peraeon, narrowly
connected to peraeonal segment I. Lateral edges
of body parallel for most of length.

Segments I-IV produced anteriorly. Segment I

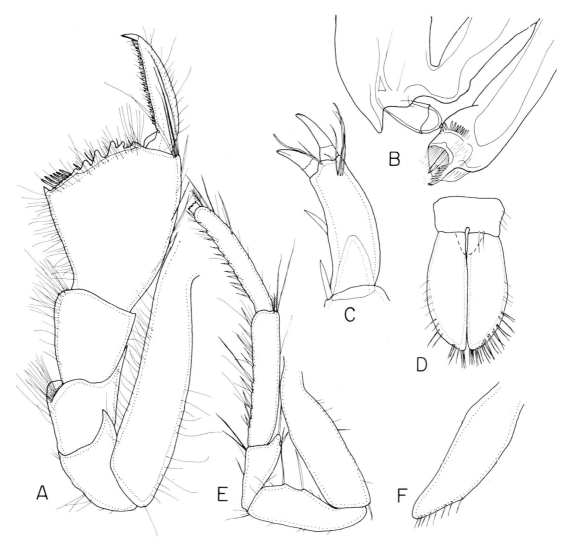

Fig. 22. Stenetrium inflectofrons n. sp. (paratype male, 8 mm long): A, male peraeopod I; B, male pleopod 2; C, dactylus of peraeopod VII; D, male pleopods 1; E, peraeopod II; F, exopod of maxilliped.

longest, about twice as long as segment IV; segment IV shortest of all; coxal plates show on lateral margins of III and IV and obscurely on II. Segments V-VII with lateral borders subquadrate, produced slightly posteriorly. Coxal plates show on posterior borders of V.

Pleotelson about as long as wide with some small teeth and with small posterolateral notches, posterior margin evenly rounded. Anterolateral point on segment 1 of antenna 2 obscure. Antennal squama on segment 3 shorter than both length and breadth of segment. Manus of peraeopod I missing from type specimen (see remarks section below). Basis of peraeopod I about two and one-half times length of basis on peraeopods II-VII.

Measurements. Holotype male, 11 mm long;

paratype male, 8 mm long; immature female, 2.5 mm long.

Derivation of name. 'Inflectofrons' comes from the Latin 'inflecto,' meaning bent, and 'frons,' meaning front. It refers to the angular nature or bend of the anterolateral processes in relation to the main part of the cephalon.

Type locality. Vema station 18-8; South Atlantic on slope east of Cabo San Antonio, Argentina; 36°06'S, 53°18'W; February 4, 1962; 278-282 m.

Distribution. The species also was collected at three Eltanin stations in the Scotia Sea between Burdwood Bank and the Falkland Islands: Sta. 6-339; start at 53°05'S, 59°31'W; 512 m; finish at 53°08'S, 59°24'W; 586 m; December 3, 1962; one

Fig. 23. Stenetrium magnimanum n. sp.: A, holotype male (8.5 mm long); B-F, male pleopods 1-5, respetively; G, male peraeopod I, H, antenna 2 peduncle.

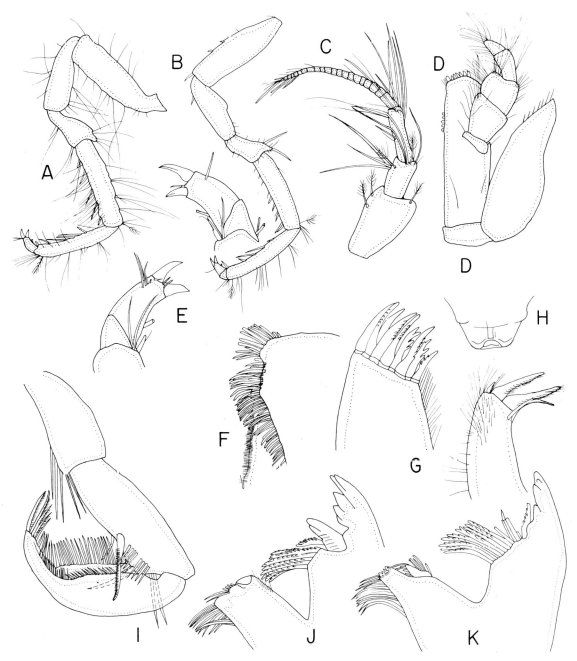

Fig. 24. Stenetrium magnimanum n. sp.: A, peraeopod VII; B, peraeopod II wth detail of
dactylus; C, antenna 1; D, maxilliped; E, dactylus of peraeopod VII; F, hypopharynx;
G, maxilla 1; H, labrum; I, mandibular palp; J, left mandible; K, right mandible.

male 8 mm long. Sta. 6-340; start at 53°07.6'S, 59°23.2'W; 578 m; finish at 53°06.7'S, 59°21.1'W; 567 m; December 3, 1962; two females 8.5 and 3.5 mm long. Sta. 11-980; east entrance to Strait of Magellan; start at 52°30'S, 67°14'W; 82 m; finish at 52°31'S, 67°14'W; 82 m; February 14, 1964; one immature female.

Affinities. Stenetrium haswelli Beddard has a very similar general body configuration, but lacks posterolateral notches on the pleotelson. The length of peraeopod I, the lateral margins of peraeonal segment II, and the posterior margin of the pleotelson are all apparently different in the two species. Male peraeopods I are very similar in length and general configuration, but the palms are very different. Stenetrium inflectfrons and

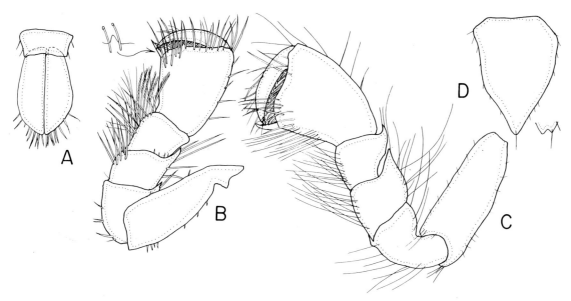

Fig. 25. Stenetrium magnimanum n. sp.: A, male pleopods 1, juvenile; B, small male peraeopod I; C, female peraeopod I; D, female pleopod 2 (sympod).

S. haswelli Beddard were found close to one another at stations. Beddard's illustration (which is unclear in many details) might be mistaken in some aspects, and the two species are perhaps the same. They are considered separate here because of the many morphological differences which seem to be apparent, but a look at Beddard's specimen might reveal more similarities.

Remarks. On the male specimen of S. inflectofrons from station 6-339, the palm of the manus has a unique armature. It is the only species of the genus which has both bladelike teeth which are extensions of the edge of the palm and spinelike teeth as well.

Stenetrium magnimanum n. sp.
Figs. 23A-23H, 24A-24K and 25A-25D

Diagnosis. Manus of peraeopod I with two large teeth of special configuration on edge of palm.

Description. Many ocelli. Cephalon with acutely pointed inwardly curved anterolateral processes and small but sharply pointed frontal processes. Rostrum triangular, apex rounded, length about as long as width of base. Peraeonal segment I largest with produced anterolateral borders and lateral borders with large grooved coxal processes. Lateral margins of segments II-IV straight, coxal processes not found or obscured in dorsal view. Pleotelson with smooth lateral margins; posterolateral notches present and only small uropodal indentations on each side of evenly rounded posterior margin.

Peduncular segment 1 of antenna 2 minutely produced. Propodus of male peraeopod I wider than long; palm broad with two large bladelike processes opposite each other. Dactylus extends beyond terminal spine on palm.

Measurements. Holotype male, 8.5 mm long; allotype female, 7 mm long; 13 paratype males, from 5 to 8 mm long; paratype females, 5-8 mm long (two 6.5-mm-long females gravid; one with 34 embryos).

Derivation of name. 'Magnimanum,' from the Latin, refers to the large hand on the manus of the specimen.

Type locality. False Bay, South Africa; 34°19'S, 18°30'E; 52 m; February 23, 1957; sand and shells (UCT TRA 138T).

Affinities. The species is very much like S. armatum, but there are some differences in the general shape of the cephalon, the peraeonal segment with coxal processes showing, and the lateral margin of the pleotelson, not to mention the obvious differences in male peraeopod I. Stenetrium magnimanum n. sp. is also somewhat like S. crassimanum, also from South Africa (see affinities section under S. crassimanum).

Stenetrium pulchrum n. sp.
Figs. 26A-26I and 27A-27L

Diagnosis. Rostrum short, rectangular; cephalon narrower than body with parallel lateral margins.

Description. Eyes with many small ocelli. Anterolateral projections acutely pointed. Large obtuse frontal processes which are broad and slightly longer than anterolateral projections. Rostrum rectangular, broader than long, placed below slightly convex anterior cephalon margin. Lateral margins of cephalon evenly rounded from anterolateral spine to posterior margin. Anterolateral margin of peraeonal segment I acutely pointed, next three peraeonal segments less pointed. Coxal processes visible on peraeonal segments I-IV. Lateral margins of

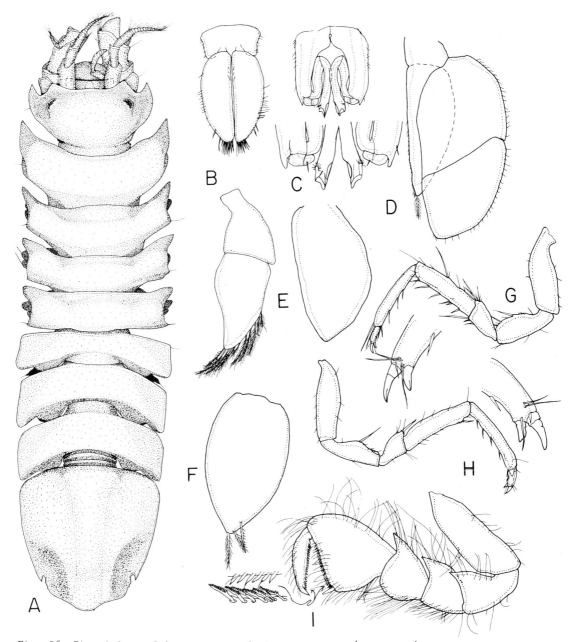

Fig. 26. _Stenetrium pulchrum_ n. sp.: A, holotype male (9 mm long); B, male pleopods 1; C, male pleopods 2 (two views); D-F, pleopods 3-5, respectively; G, peraeopod III with detail of dactylus; H, peraeopod VII with detail of dactylus; I, peraeopod I with detail of palm and dactylus.

peraeonal segments V-VII subquadrate and smooth. Pleotelson longer than broad with deeply set posterolateral grooves and well-defined posterolateral spines. Posterior margin obtusely rounded, with only slight indentations for uropodal bases.

Peraeopod I with propodus longer than wide with small teeth on palm and on inner margin of dactylus. Dactylus extended only slightly beyond terminal palmar spine. Unguis larger of two

dactyl terminal claws on peraeopods II-VII. Only one interior dactyl claw. Very narrow endopod on pleopod 3.

Measurements. Holotype male, 9 mm long; allotype female, 5 mm long; fragments, sex undetermined.

Derivation of name. 'Pulchrum,' from the Latin 'pulcher' (for beautiful), refers to the beautiful symmetry of the species.

Type locality. _Vema_ station 15-131; slope east

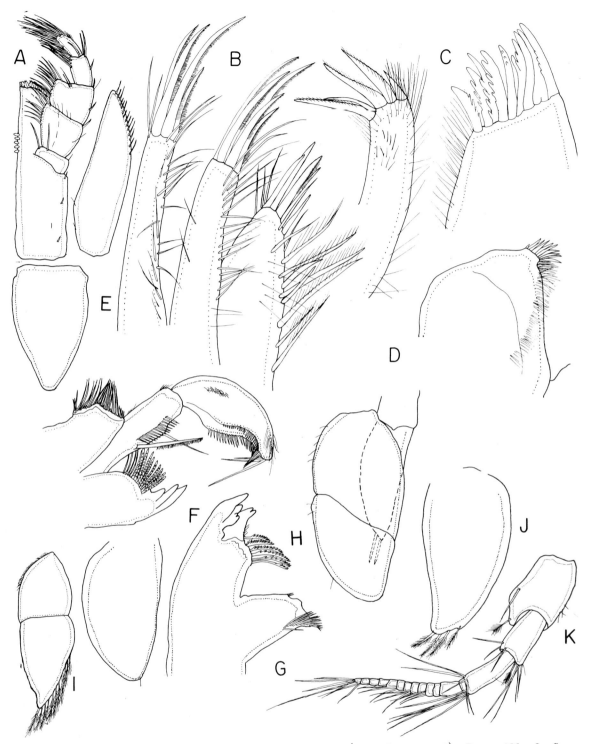

Fig. 27. Stenetrium pulchrum n. sp.: A, maxilliped (exopod reversed); B, maxilla 2; C, maxilla 1; D, hypopharynx; E, female pleopod 2 (sympod); F, right mandible; G, left mandible; H-J, female pleopods 3-5, respectively; K, antenna 1 male.

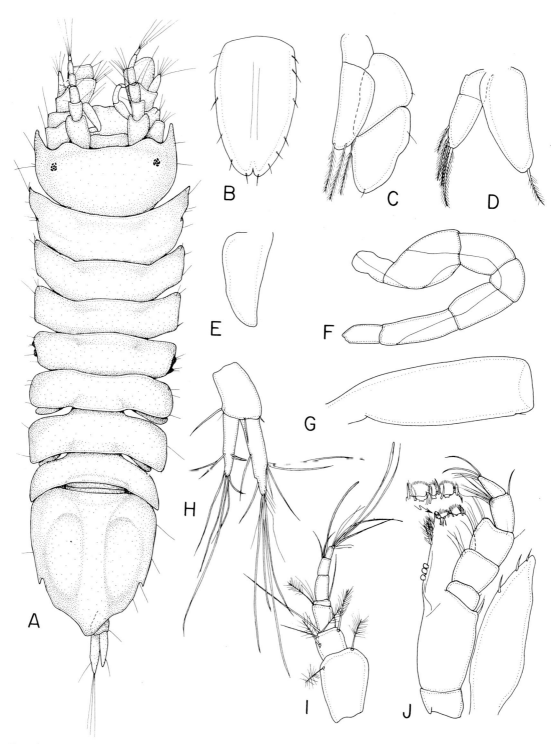

Fig. 28. *Stenetrium virginale* n. sp.: A, holotype immature female (3.5 mm long); B-E, female pleopods 2-5, respectively; F, immature peraeopod VII; G, basis of peraeopod I; H, uropod; I, antenna 1; J, maxilliped.

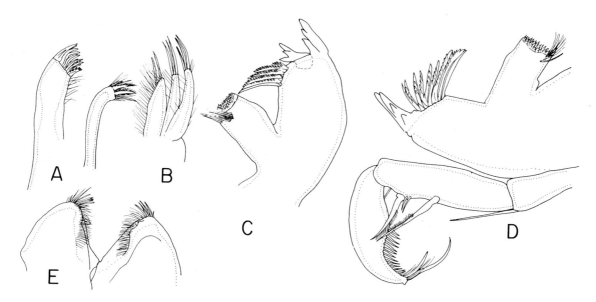

Fig. 29. Stenetrium virginale n. sp.: A, maxilla 1; B, maxilla 2; C, left mandible; D, right mandible; E, hypopharynx.

of Cabo San Antonio, Argentina; 40°14.6'S, 55°24.7'W; April 3, 1959; 1479 m.

Distribution. Specimens were also taken at Vema station 15-132 nearby the type locality; 39°57.5'S, 54°49.5'W; April 3, 1959; 1911 m; one male 5 mm long; six females 5.5-10 mm long; 10-mm-long female gravid.

Affinities. The new species is like S. inflectofrons, but differs from it in the structure of the cephalon, the ocelli number and shape, the shape of the pleotelson, and in many other details such as the number of spines on the propodus of peraeopod II.

Stenetrium virginale n. sp.
Figs. 28A-28J and 29A-29E

Diagnosis. Shape of frontal margin of cephalon with large rounded frontal processes and small eyes unique.

Description. (This description is based on an immature female.) Eyes of few ocelli. Anterolateral angles narrow, longer than obtuse or rounded frontal processes. Rostrum much wider than broad; clypeus with slightly concave frontal margin. Peraeonal segment I pointed anteriorly. Coxal process obscurely indicated only on segment IV and showing on segments V and VI. Pleotelson longer than wide with smooth edges and long posterolateral spines. Body margins generally tapering together posteriorly, including pleotelson; pleotelson ends on elongate rounded produced posterior margin.

Antenna 2 without spine on article 1. Only five flagellar articles visible on antenna 1. Very few plumose setae on pleopods 3 and 4, none on 5. Female pleopod 2 tapered to bifurcate tip. Three

coupling hooks on maxilliped, with only three setae other than two large tooth setae, on article 2 of palp.

Measurements. Holotype immature female, 3.5 mm long.

Type locality. Eltanin station 6-340; Scotia Sea between Burdwood Bank and the Falkland Islands; start at 53°07.6'S, 59°23.2'W; 578 m; finish at 53°06.7'S, 59°21.1'W; 567 m; December 3, 1962.

Distribution. Another immature female with undeveloped peraeopods VII, most probably of this species, was collected north of the Antarctic Peninsula; thus the species is found between southern South America and Antartica. Eltanin station 12-1003; start at 62°41'S, 54°43'W; 210 m; finish at 62°41'S, 54°43'W; 220 m; one immature female.

Affinities. All characters plus the lack of fully developed peraeopods VII indicate that the specimen on which the description is based was an immature female. It was, however, so different from immature specimens of other species that it is here considered as a new species.

Tenupedunculus n. g.

Description of genus. Eyeless. Trapezoidally shaped cephalon with small frontal processes and very narrow anterolateral processes on longest edge. Rostrum short, much broader than long, with concave frontal margin. Basal four articles of antenna 2 much longer when compared with length of cephalon than in other species of Stenetriidae. Body outline with lateral margin from peraeonal segment I to posterolateral notch of pleotelson subparallel; posterior margin of pleotelson evenly

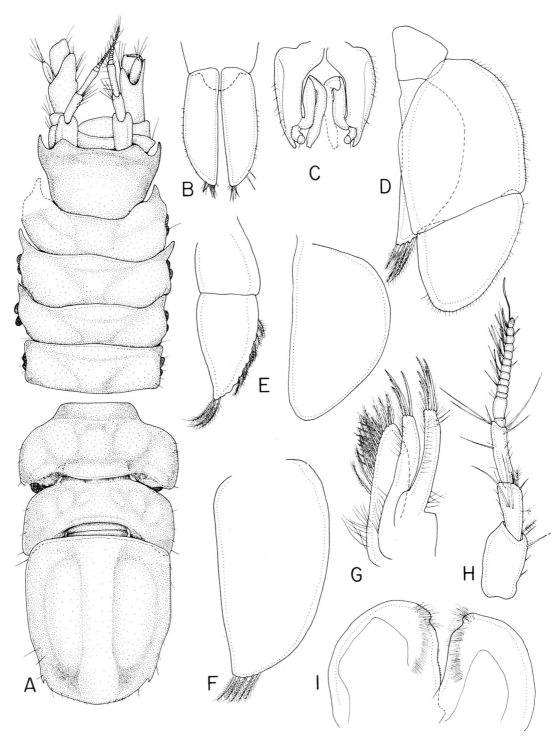

Fig. 30. _Tenupedunculus elongatus_ n. g., n. sp.: A, holotype male (12 mm long); B-F, male pleopods 1-5, respectively; G, maxilla 2; H, antenna 1; I, hypopharynx.

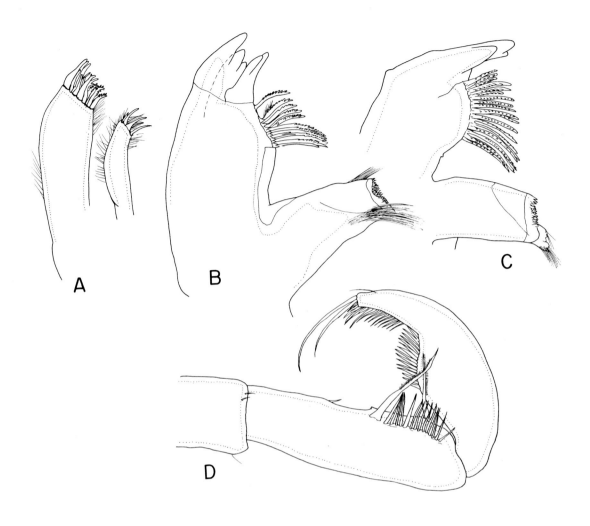

Fig. 31. _Tenupedunculus_ _elongatus_ n. g., n. sp.: A, maxilla 1; B, left mandible; C, right mandible; D, mandibular palp.

rounded. Anterolateral processes of segments I-III abruptly narrowed with rounded tips. Coxal processes show in dorsal view on segments I-IV. Male pleopods 2 and others _Stenetrium_-like. (The manus and uropods are missing from the type specimen.)

Etymology and gender. 'Tenu,' from the Latin tenuis, meaning thin, and 'pedunculus,' meaning foot, are combined. The latter is used as in botany to mean stalk and refers to the elongate base, or peduncle, of the antennae. The gender is masculine.

Affinities. The species is unique among the Stenetriidae, indeed the Stenetrioidea, in being without eyes. Also the general configuration of the body in dorsal view is different from other species. It also has especially elongate segments on the peduncle of antenna 2. The male pleopods, however, leave little doubt that the species is a

member of the Stenetriidae, being very much like those in the species of _Stenetrium_.

Type species _Tenupedunculus_ _elongatus_
n. g., n. sp.
Tenupedunculus _elongatus_ n. g., n. sp.
Figs. 30A-30I and 31A-31D

Diagnosis. Eyeless. General elongate body configuration unique.

Description. Eyeless. Anterolateral processes very short and narrow, only slightly longer than obtuse frontal processes. Rostrum broader than long. Cephalon subquadrate or trapezoidal, narrower than peraeonal segments.

Anterolateral margins of peraeonal segments I-III each with anterolateral borders abruptly narrowed to spinelike point. Coxal processes visible on lateral edges of segments I-IV. Segment

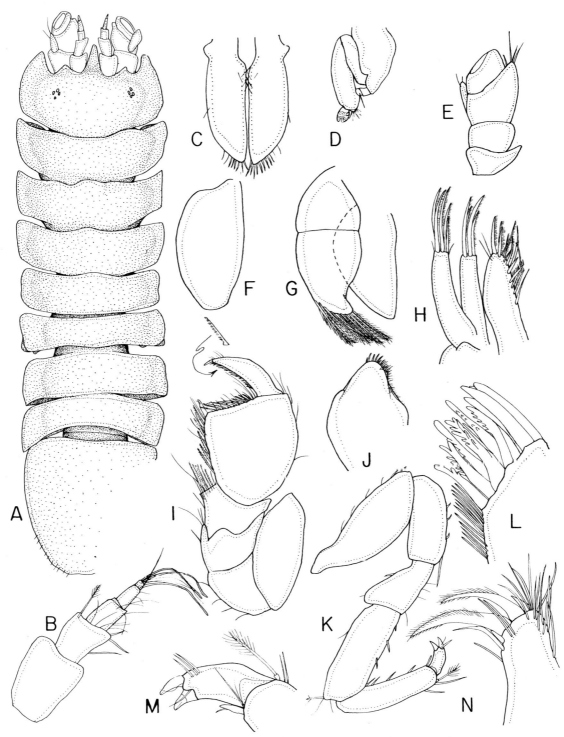

Fig. 32. Stenetrigus syzygus (Barnard, 1940) n. g.: A, male (5 mm long); B, antenna 1;
C and D, male pleopods 1 and 2, respectively; E, antenna 2 peduncle; F and G, pleopods
5 and 4, respectively; H, maxilla 2; I, male peraeopod I; J, hypopharynx; K, peraeopod
II; L, maxilla 1 exopod; M, detail, peraeopod II; N, maxilla 1 endopod.

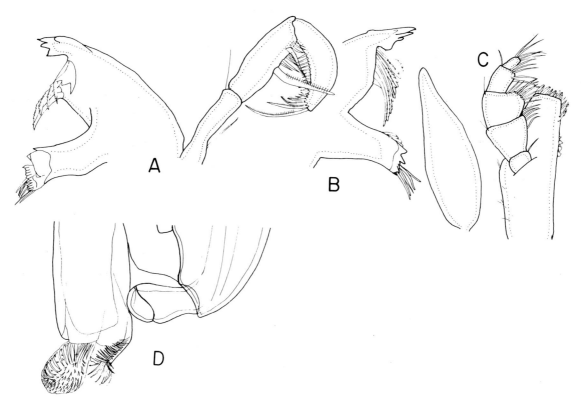

Fig. 33. Stenetrigus syzygus (Barnard, 1940) n. g.: A, left mandible; B, right mandible; C, maxilliped; D, detail, male pleopod 2.

V destroyed; VI and VII with posterolateral margins produced. (The coxal processes probably would be obscured if the peraeonal segments were not distorted by preservation of the specimen.)

Pleotelson longer than broad with smooth lateral margins and small posterolateral angles. Posterior margin evenly rounded, without indications of uropodal bases.

Antenna 2 without spine segment 2; pedunculur segments 1-4 greatly elongate. Squama of antenna 2 about as long as segment 3 is wide and about half as long as length of segment. Male pleopod with same general configurations as in other species of Stenetriidae. Peraeopods missing.

Measurements. Holotype male, 12 mm long.

Derivation of name. 'Elongatus' refers to the elongate nature of the antennae of the species.

Type locality. Vema station 17-84; southwestern part of Argentine Basin; 50°15'S, 35°53'W; 4696 m; June 1, 1961.

Stenetrigus n. g.

Description of genus. Eyes with few ocelli (type species with four). Male pleopod 2 apparently without fused sympod (absent or not visible); only two rami present, coming directly from sternum. Apparently this is true for both male and female [Barnard, 1940, p. 433]. No posterolateral notch on edge of pleotelson. Long anterolateral processes and moderately long frontal processes on frontal border; rostrum longer than broad and acutely pointed. Manus simple, toothed, and with plumose setae on ventral margin of propodus.

Etymology and gender. The name is arbitrarily derived from Stenetrium, the type genus of Stenetriidae. The gender is masculine.

Type species Stenetrium syzygus Barnard, 1940
Stenetrigus syzygus (Barnard)
Figs. 32A-32N and 33A-33D

Stenetrium syzygus Barnard, 1940, p. 432, figs. 20a-20f.--Wolff, 1962, p. 24.

Diagnosis. Eyes small; lateral margins broadly rounded; no coxal extensions on peraeonal segments I-IV.

Description. Eyes of only four ocelli. Lateral borders of cephalon regularly curved, and include anterolateral processes. Frontal margin with two obtuse frontal processes and long (slightly longer than anterolateral processes), acutely pointed rostrum. Body with parallel edges; peraeonal segments I-IV without anterior flare of anterolateral angles or posterior flare on segments V-VIII. Posterolateral notches of pleotelson absent; small spines on lateral margins.

Antenna 1 with flagellum of 3 articles. Peduncular segment 1 of antenna 2 not showing in dorsal view. Merus of male peraeopod I with spined setae on ventral margin; carpus also with such setae. No inferior dactyl spine on dactyli of peraeopod II-VII.

Measurements. Male, 5 mm long.

Type locality. Still Bay, South Africa; one gravid and one nongravid female [Barnard, 1940].

Distribution. Still Bay to Knysna, South Africa; Knysna estuary (UCT KNY 171S); one male 5 mm long; littoral on substrate of rocks.

Affinities. If the pleopods are as described (the same in male and female), then the species is unique among the Stenetriidae. There are major differences--presence of female pleopod 1 and presence of nonfused sympod--which set the species apart from other Stenetriidae. When more specimens, both male and female, are collected and examined, the genus might be placed in a new family because of the peculiar pleopods.

Remarks. Barnard [1940] stated that male pleopod 1 had very short peduncles which were fused. He did not illustrate them well. In the specimen examined here the peduncles did not seem to be fused. Indeed, the two rami composing the pleopods seemed to be completely free from each other and connected directly to the body. Apparently then the sympod is very small or absent. It is also of extraordinary interest to note that pleopods 1 in both male and female are the same. Barnard stated that Monod confirmed his observations on this point, but unfortunately only one male specimen was available for observation for this study. It was not dissected.

Asellote Isopod Stations

Stations listed are the ship stations where isopods were caught. Latitude and longitude indicate the positions, and in the case of the Eltanin and Hero stations, they indicate the positions at the beginning and at the end of the trawls.

Challenger Stations

Station 320. (37°17'S, 53°52'W); Stenetrium haswelli Beddard.

Eltanin Stations

Station 6-339. (53°05'S, 59°31'W; 53°08'S, 59°24'W); Stenetrium inflectofrons n. sp.

Station 6-340. (53°07.6'S, 59°23.2'W; 53°06.7'S, 59°21.1'W); Stenetrium inflectofrons n. sp.

Station 6-410. (61°18'S, 56°09'W, 69°20'S, 56°10'W); Stenetrium acutum Vanhöffen.

Station 6-418. (62°38.9'S, 56°10.2'W; 62°39.9'S, 56°07.8'W); Stenetrium acutum Vanhöffen.

Station 6-430. (62°38'S, 59°37'W; 60°41'S, 59°23'W); Stenetrium acutum Vanhöffen.

Station 9-740. (56°6.2'S, 66°19'W; 56°06.5'S, 66°30'W); Stenetrium beddardi Kussakin.

Station 11-980. (52°30'S, 67°14'W; 52°31'S, 67°14'W); Stenetrium inflectofrons n. sp.

Station 11-1003. (62°41'S, 54°43'W; 62°41'S, 54°43'W); Stenetrium acutum Vanhöffen; Stenetrium virginale n. sp.

Galathea Stations

Station 602. (43°58'S, 165°25'E); Stenetrium abyssale Wolff.

Station 664. (36°34'S, 178°57'W); Stenetrium abyssale Wolff.

Hero Stations

Station 715-895. (54°59.9'S, 64°50'W; 55°00'S, 64°47.5'W); Protallocoxa drakensis n. sp.

Ob Stations

Station 203. (66°12'04"S, 57°42'02"E); Stenetrium acutum Vanhöffen.

Station 479. (45°16'S, 54°54'W); Stenetrium beddardi Kussakin; Stenetrium dentimanum Kussakin.

Station 480. (43°41'S, 59°34'W); Stenetrium beddardi Kussakin; Stenetrium dentimanum Kussakin.

Vema Stations

Station 14-74. (34°05.5'S, 18°06'E); Stenetrium saldanha Barnard.

Station 15-131. (40°14.6'S, 55°24.7'W); Stenetrium pulchrum n. sp.

Station 15-132. (39°57.5'S, 54°49.5'W); Stenetrium pulchrum n. sp.

Station 17-84. (50°15'S, 35°53'W); Tenupedunculus elongatus n. g., n. sp.

Station 17-99. (44°25'S, 59°19'W); Stenetrium acutum Vanhöffen.

Station 17-101. (38°13'S, 55°19'W); Stenetrium acutum Vanhöffen.

Station 18-8. (36°06'S, 53°18'W); Stenetrium inflectofrons n. sp.

APPENDIX: SUMMARY OF SPECIES DISCUSSED AND DISPOSITION OF TYPE SPECIMENS

TABLE A1. Species of Superfamilies Protallocoxoidea (Family Protallocoxidae) and Stenetrioidea (Family Stenetriidae) From the Antarctic and Southern Seas

	Maximum Length, mm	Depth, m	Type Locality[a]	Geographic Range
Family Protallocoxidae[a]				
P. drakensis n. sp.	9	438-548	Hero 715-895	Off tip of South America
Family Stenetriidae				
Described Species[b]				
S. abyssale Wolff, 1962	9.9	4510-4540	Galathea 664	Kermadec Trench, northeastern New Zealand
S. acutum Vanhöffen, 1914	12	150-3397	Gauss Station	Circum-Antarctic
S. armatum Haswell, 1881	12.7	littoral	Port Jackson	Southeastern Australia
S. bartholomei Barnard, 1940	6.5	littoral	Still Bay	Cape Town to Mbotyi, South Africa
S. beddardi Kussakin, 1967	9.55	479-680	Ob 479	Drake Passage and 1000 km northeast of Falkland Islands
S. crassimanum Barnard, 1914	7	littoral	St. James, False Bay	Off Cape Penisula
S. dagama Barnard, 1920	7.5	420	30 km off Cape Point	30 km off Cape Point South Africa
S. dalmeida Barnard, 1920	7.5	420	80 km off Cape Point	80 km off Cape Point South Africa
S. dentimanum Kussakin, 1967	11.6	479-680	Ob 480	1000 km northeast of Falkland Islands
S. diazi Barnard, 1920	6	littoral	Buffel's Bay	Buffel's Bay, South Africa
S. fractum Chilton, 1884	4.2	littoral	Lyttelton Harbour	Lyttelton Harbour, New Zealand
S. glauerti Nicholls, 1929	5	littoral	Bathurst Point, Rottnest Island	Western Australia, near Perth
S. haswelli Beddard, 1886	16	1097	Challenger 320	Argentine Basin, off Río de la Plata
S. macrochirum Nicholls, 1929	5.9	littoral	Dongarra, western Australia	Western Australia, near Perth
S. rotundatum Vanhöffen, 1914	8.5	385	Gauss Station	Davis Sea, off Antarctica
S. saldanha Barnard, 1920	7	0-246	115 km off Cape St. Blaize	Cape Point to Cape Seal, South Africa
S. spinirostrum Nicholls, 1929	5.8	littoral	Bathurst Point Rottnest Island	Western Australia, near Perth
S. truncatum Nicholls, 1929	5.5	littoral	Bathurst Point Rottnest Island	Western Australia, near Perth
New Species[b]				
S. esquartum n. sp.	5.5	littoral	False Bay	False Bay to Oolora, South Africa
S. inflectofrons n. sp.	11	80-588	Vema 18-8	Scotia Sea between Burdwood Bank and Falkland Islands
S. magnimanum n. sp.	8.5	littoral	False Bay	False Bay, South Africa
S. pulchrum n. sp.	10	1479-1911	Vema 15-131	Slope east of Cabo San Antonio, Argentina
S. virginale n. sp.	3.5	220-567	Eltanin 340	Scotia Sea To Antarctic Peninsula
New Genera[c]				
Tenupedunculus n. g. elongatus n. sp.	12	4696	Vema 17-84	Southeastern part of Argentine Basin
Stenetrigus n. g. syzygus (Barnard, 1940)	5	littoral	Still Bay	Still Bay to Knysna, South Africa

aType genus Protallocoxa Schultz, 1978.
bType genus Stenetrium Haswell, 1881.
cType genus Tenupedunculus n. g. and type genus Stenetrigus n. g.

TABLE A2. Disposition of Type Specimens

Species	Type	Location	Repository
Stenetrium esquartum	holotype male, allotype female, paratypes	False Bay, South Africa	UCT FAL 172V
Stenetrium inflectofrons	holotype male	Vema 18-8	AMNH 12591
	paratype male	Eltanin (USC) 339	AHF 6211a
	paratype female	Eltanin (USC) 340	AHF 6211a
	nontype	Eltanin (USC) 980	AHF (no number)
Stenetrium magnimanum	holotype male, allotype female, paratypes	False Bay, South Africa	UCT TRA 138T
Stenetrium pulchrum	holotype male	Vema 15-131	AMNH 12587
	allotype female	Vema 15-131	AMNH 12588
	paratype female	Vema 15-131	AMNH 12589
	nontype	Vema 15-132	AMNH 12590
Stenetrium virginale	holotype female	Eltanin (USC) 340	AHF 6210
	nontype female	Eltanin (USC) 1003	AHF (no number)
Tenupedunculus elongatus	holotype male	Vema 17-84	AMNH 12595
Protallocoxa drakensis	holotype female	Hero 715-895	USNM 171447

AHF, Allan Hancock Foundation; AMNH, American Museum of Natural History; UCT, University of Cape Town Museum; USNM, National Museum of Natural History.

Acknowledgments. This work was supported for the most part by the Smithsonian Oceanographic Sorting Center's program, 'Cooperative systematics and analyses of polar biological materials,' through a National Science Foundation grant DDP 76-23979, B. J. Landrum, Principal Investigator. The specimens from the University of Cape Town Museum were kindly sent for study through John H. Day and John Field. The specimens from the Australian Museum were kindly obtained through the aid of John C. Yaldwin, formerly of that museum.

References

Barnard, K. H.
  1914   Contributions to the crustacean fauna of South Africa. 1. Additions to the marine Isopoda. Ann. S. Afr. Mus., 10(11): 197-230.
  1920   Contributions to the crustacean fauna of South Africa. 6. Further additions to the list of marine Isopoda. Ann. S. Afr. Mus., 17(11): 319-438.
  1940   Contributions to the crustacean fauna of South Africa. 9. Further additions to the Tanaidacea, Isopoda, and Amphipoda, together with keys for the identification of hitherto recorded marine and freshwater species. Ann. S. Afr. mus., 32(5): 381-543.
Beddard, F. E.
  1886a Preliminary notice of the Isopoda collected during the voyage of H.M.S. Challenger. 3. Proc. Zool. Soc. London, part 1: 97-122.
  1886b Report on the Isopoda collected by H.M.S. Challenger during the years 1873-1876. 2. Challenger Rep. 17: 1-178.
Chilton, C.
  1884   Additions to the sessil-eyed Crustacea of New Zealand. Trans. Proc. N. Z. Inst., 16(14): 249-265.
Hale, H. M.
  1929   The Crustaceans of South Australia. Part III, pp. 201-308. British Science Guild (South Australian Branch), Adelaide.
Hansen, H. J.
  1905   On the morphology and classification of the Asellota-group of crustaceans, with descriptions of the genus Stenetrium Hasw. and its species. Proc. Zool. Soc. London (1904), 2: 302-331.
Haswell, W. A.
  1881   On some new Austrlian marine Isopoda, 1. Proc. Linn. Soc. N. S. W., 5(4): 470-581.
  1882   Catalogue of the Australian stalk- and sessile-eyed crustacea,, pp. 1-324. Australian Museum, F. W. White, Sydney.
  1885   A revision of the Australian Isopoda. Proc. Linn. Soc. N. S. W. (1884), 9: 1001-1015.
Hurley, D. E.
  1961   A checklist and key to the Crustacea Isopoda of New Zealand and the subantarctic islands. Trans. R. Soc. N. Z., 1(20): 259-292.
Kensley, B.
  1975   Marine Isopoda from the continental shelf of South Africa. Ann. S. Afr. Mus., 67(4): 35-89.

1976   Isopodan and tanaidacean Crustacea from
        the St. Paul and Amsterdam Islands,
        southern Indian Ocean. Ann. S. Afr.
        Mus., 69(11): 261-323.
Kussakin, O. G.
1967   Fauna of Isopoda and Tanaidacea in the
        coastal zones of the Antarctic and sub-
        antarctic waters. Studies of marine
        fauna, 4(13). Biol. Rep. Sov. Antarctic
        Exped. (1955-1958), 3: 220-389.
Menzies, R. J. and P. W. Glynn
1968   The common marine isopod Crustacea of
        Puerto Rico: A handbook for marine
        biologists. Stud. Fauna Curacao, 27:
        1-133.
Miller, M. A.
1941   The isopod Crustacea of the Hawaiian
        Islands. 2. Asellota. Occ. Pap. Bernice
        P. Bishop Mus., 16(13): 305-320.
Monod, T.
1933   Mission Robert-Ph. Dollfus en Egypte.
        Tanaidacea et Isopoda. Mem. Inst.
        Egypte, 21: 16-264.
Nicholls, G. E.
1929   Some new species of Stenetrium from wes-
        tern Australia. Proc. Linn. Soc. N. S.
        W., 54: 361-374.
Nierstrasz, H. F.
1941   Die Isopoden der Siboga-Expedition. 4.
        Isopoda Genuina. 3. Gnathiidea, Anthuri-
        dea, Valvifera, Asellota, Phreatoici-
        dea. In Siboga-Exped. Monogr., 32(Supl
        d): 235-308. Brill, Leiden, Netherlands.
Nobili, G.
1906   Diagnoses preliminaries de crustaces,
        decapodes et isopodes nouveau recueillis
        par M. le Dr. G. Seurat aux Iles Touamo-
        tou. Bull. Mus. Hist. Nat. Paris, 5:
        256-270.

1907   Ricerche sui crostacei della Polinesia.
        Decapodi, stomatopodi, anisopodi e iso-
        podi. Memorie Accad. Sci., Torino, Ser.
        2, 57: 351-430.
Nordenstam, A.
1933   Marine Isopoda of the families Seroli-
        dae, Idotheidae, Pseudidotheidae, Arc-
        turidae, Parasellidae and Stenetriidae

mainly from the south Atlantic. Further
        Zool. Results Swedish Antarctic Exped.,
        1901-1903, 3(1): 1-284.
1946   Marine Isopoda from Professor Dr. Sixten
        Bock's Pacific Expedition 1917-1918.
        Ark. Zool., Ser. A. 37(7): 1-31.
Richardson, H.
1902   The marine and terrestrial isopods of
        the Bermudas, with descriptions of new
        genera and species. Trans. Conn. Acad.
        Arts Sci., 11: 277-310.
Schultz, G. A.
1969   How to know the marine isopod crusta-
        ceans. In Pictured-key nature ser.,
        vii-359. William Brown, Dubuque, Iowa.
1976   Species of asellotes (Isopoda: Parasel-
        loidea) from Anvers Island, Antarctica.
        In D. L. Pawson (Ed.), Biology of the
        antarctic seas VI, Antarctic Res. Ser.,
        26: 1-25. AGU, Washington, D.C.
1978   Protallocoxoidea new superfamily (Isopo-
        da Asellota) with a description of
        Protallocoxa weddellensis new genus, new
        species from the Antarctic Ocean. Crus-
        taceana, 34(3): 245-250.
1979   Aspects of the evolution and origin of
        the deep-sea isopod crustaceans. Sarsia,
        64: 77-83.
Stebbing, T. R. R.
1905   Report on the Isopoda collected by Pro-
        fessor Herdman, at Ceylon, in 1902. Cey-
        lon Pearl Oyster Fish. Suppl. Rep. 23:
        1-64. Roy. Soc. London.
Vanhöffen, E.
1914   Die Isopoden der Deutschen
        Südpolar-Expedition 1901-1903. Dt. Südp-
        pol. Exped., 20: 449-598.
Whitelegge, T.
1889   List of the marine and fresh-water
        invertebrate fauna of Port Jackson and
        neighbourhood. J. Proc. R. Soc. N. S.
        W., 23(2): 163-323.
Wolff, T.
1962   The systematics and biology of bathyal
        and abyssal Isopoda Asellota. Galathea
        Rep., 6: 1-320.

ARCTURIDAE FROM THE ANTARCTIC AND SOUTHERN SEAS (ISOPODA, VALVIFERA) PART I

George A. Schultz

Hampton, New Jersey 08827

Abstract. This is the first of several papers on the Arcturidae from the Antarctic and southern seas based on material collected by the research vessels Eltanin, Hero, and Islas Orcadas and other smaller collections and supplied by the Smithsonian Oceanographic Sorting Center. Two species from the shakedown cruise of the Hero to the Arctic are included. The paper contains descriptions of two new species and six new genera. Thirteen formerly described species are included with six redescriptions based on new specimens or reexamination of specimens of known species. All species are illustrated or re-illustrated where specimens were available. A map of the distribution of the species from Antarctic waters is included. A total of 23 species is recorded.

Introduction

This is the first of several papers on the Arcturidae from the Antarctic and southern seas, and it contains descriptions of ten new species and six new genera. Thirteen formerly described species are included with six redescriptions based on new specimens or reexamination of old specimens. All species are illustrated or re-illustrated where specimens were available. A total of 23 species is recorded (Appendix 2), and distribution in Antarctic waters is recorded on Map 1.

At least 75 species of arcturids are present in the Antarctic and southern seas. They formerly have been included mainly in Antarcturus zur Strassen (1902, 1903) and Microarcturus Nordenstam (1933), but these two genera are very broadly defined. One of the objects of this study is to begin to redescribe some of the known species and new species as they are encountered and place them in a more logical, less broadly defined set of genera, based on new criteria. The work is based on collections made by the personnel of the research vessels Eltanin, Hero, and Islas Orcadas and other small collections made available to me through the Smithsonian Oceanographic Sorting Center. A complete classification of the Arcturidae from the Antarctic and southern seas will be given in a latter part of this work now in preparation. The type specimens of all new species have been placed in the National Museum of Natural History (see Appendix 3).

Arcturus Latreille

The genus was instituted by Latreille [1829] and is the type genus of the family Arcturidae. Throughout the years many species were placed in the broadly defined genus, but through revisions most were removed and placed in new genera. The species now in the genus are mainly from the Arctic and bordering northern regions with a few species from more southern locations. The diagnosis of the genus given here is mainly based on this redescription of the type species Arcturus baffini (Sabine).

Diagnosis. Cephalon and peraeonal segment I partly fused. Pleura of peraeonal segment I extended ventrally to cover posterior part of buccal mass. Cephalon and peraeonal segments I-VII with two dorsal spines on each. Pleon with two free segments; posterolateral spines absent. Peraeopod I short, not obviously gnathal; dactylus short. Peraeopods II-IV similar to peraeopod I but longer. Antenna 2 longer than body. Peraeopods V-VII short, prehensile, and with biuncinate dactyli.

Type species. Idotea baffini Sabine, 1824. The species on which the genus was established by Latreille [1829], Arcturus tuberculatus, is an objective synonym of I. baffini.

Arcturus baffini (Sabine)
Figs. 1A-1J

The species Arcturus baffini (Sabine, 1824) was collected on the shakedown cruise to the Davis Strait by the Hero. It is the type species of the type genus of Arcturidae, hence redescribed here.

Description. Eyes of moderate size, vertically subelliptical. Cephalon and peraeonal segments I-VII and pleonal segments 1 and 2 each with two dorsal spines. Body surface minutely tuberculate, with few hairlike setae on body and spines. Cephalon and peraeonal segment I partly fused with pleura of peraeonal segment I extending below pleura of cephalon. Pleon with segments 1 and 2

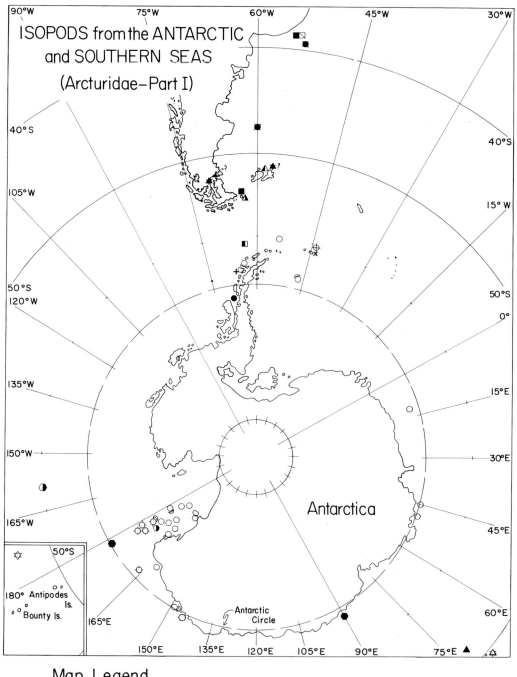

Map Legend

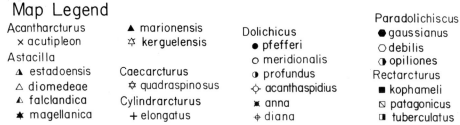

Map 1. Distribution of isopods from the Antarctic and southern seas.

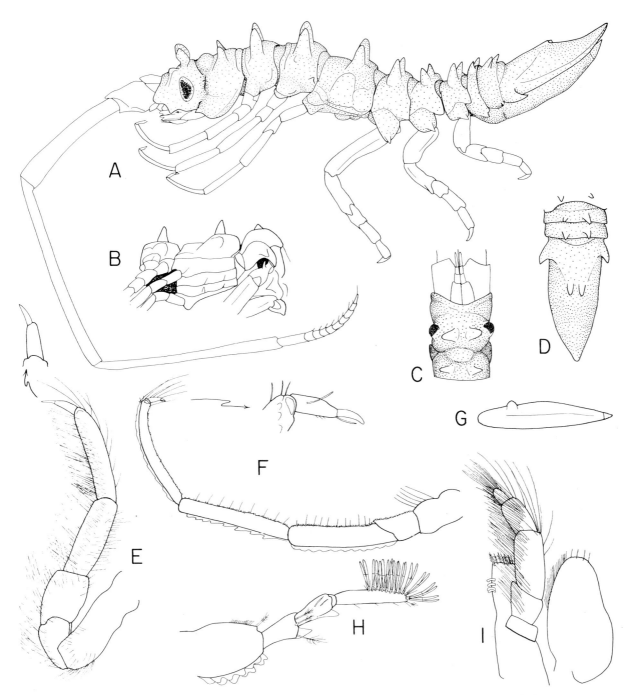

Fig. 1. Arcturus baffini (Sabine 1824). A, female 33 mm long; B, ventral oblique view peraeonal segments III-V; C, dorsal view cephalon-peraeonal segment I; D, dorsal view posterior part; E, peraeopod I; F, peraeopod II; G, valve; H, antenna 1; I, maxilliped.

free; indicated segment 3 fused, with pointed lateral spines; dorsum with two short spines; posterolateral spines lacking; posterior margin acutely pointed. Peraeonal segment IV longest but not much longer than others, with peraeopod arising from extreme anterior of segment. Coxal spines well defined on peraeonal segments V-VII and small spine on pleonal segment I.

Antenna I with peduncular segments 2 and 3 about as long as short flagellum; about 12 groups of

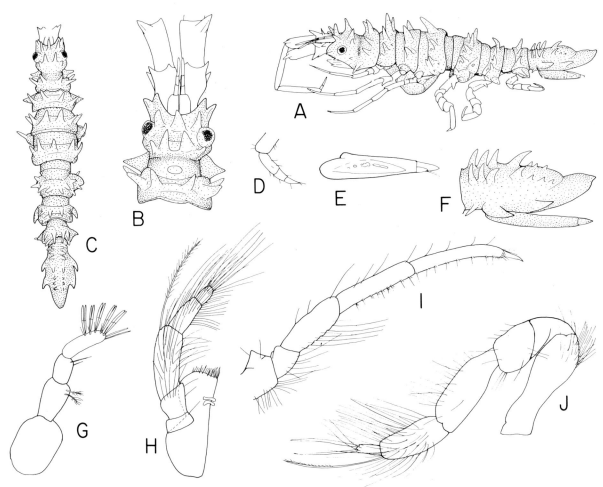

Fig. 2. <u>Spectrarcturus multispinatus</u> gen. nov., sp. nov. A, holotype gravid female 9 mm long; B, detail cephalon-peraeonal segment I; C, dorsal view holotype; D, flagellum antenna 2; E, valve; F, detail pleon; G, antenna 1; H, maxilliped; I, peraeopod II; J, peraeopod I.

aesthetasc's on flagellum. Antenna 2 much longer than body; about 10 flagellar articles (flagellum from second female illustrated). Maxilliped with narrow palp and endite; endite with four coupling hooks; exopod about half again as wide and about as long as endite, with broadly rounded apex.

Peraeopod I not obviously gnathal and about half as long as peraeopod II; dactylus and propodus like that of peraeopods II-IV; inner margins of segments, except dactylus, fringed with moderately long setae. Peraeopods II-IV with dactyli, including unguis, much shorter than long propodus; inner margins of segments, especially smooth and elongate. Female 33 mm long.

Measurements. One female to 35 mm long.

Locality. Off Little Nellefiske Bank, Greenland; Hero 3-29C; 64°54'N, 53°38'W; August 18, 1968; 79-85 m.

Distribution. A second collection was made at the same station, Hero 3-29F. The species is found over much of the Arctic Ocean.

Material. Four nongravid females ranging from 27 to 35 mm long were collected from what really is two collections at one station (two specimens were collected on each of 2 days). One of the females had a wide slit at the ventral separation between the cephalon and peraeonal segment I. This was not apparent on the specimen illustrated here.

Affinities. The relative size and pattern of dorsal spines are similar to those illustrated for A. baffini by Richardson [1905, p. 337, Figure 367]. The pleon has two free segments, and short dactyli are present on peraeopods I-IV in both sets of specimens. Antenna 2 has about ten flagellar articles in these specimens and about eight as shown by Richardson. Hairlike setae cover the body and appendages in Richardson's illustrations. The body is relatively free of hairs in the specimens recorded here.

Remarks. The species was taken at the same station as Spectrarcturus multispinatus gen. nov., sp. nov. described next.

Spectrarcturus gen. nov.

The genus is based on a species which looks much like Pleuroprion murdochi (Benedict, 1898) in dorsal ornamentation (see affinities section) but is definitely not related to Pleuroprion chuni (zur Strassen, 1902), the type species of Pleuroprion, and that is one reason why the specimens are considered to be in a new genus here.

Diagnosis. Cephalon fused to peraeonal segment I but with more than two spines on dorsum. More than two spines on dorsum of peraeonal segments II-VII. Pleon with no free segments; spines on dorsum arranged in two rows; lateral spines on indicated segment 3 and posterolateral spines prominent. Antenna 2 shorter than body; few flagellar articles. Dactylus of peraeopod I without unguis but with long apical setae.

Derivation and gender of name. The name is from the Latin 'spectrum,' which means appearance, since the species has the appearance of an Arcturus. The gender is masculine.

Type species. Spectrarcturus multispinatus sp. nov.

Spectrarcturus multispinatus sp. nov.
Figs. 2A-2I

This species has its nearest relatives in species described as members of Pleuroprion in northern regions.

Diagnosis. See generic diagnosis.

Description. (The type specimen is damaged at segments IV and V.) Moderately large laterally placed eyes. Cephalon and peraeonal segment I fused. Cephalon with large spines laterally placed just anterior to eyes; three spines between eyes; four spines behind eyes. Peraeonal segment I with six long spines; anterolateral corners large. Six spines on peraeonal segment III. Peraeonal segment IV damaged. Four large dorsal spines and two lateral spines on peraeonal segments VI and VII.

Pleon with no free segments and indications of segmentation slight; dorsum with eight long and six small spines in two rows; lateral spines on indicated third segments and posterolateral spines large. Posterior margin of pleon produced well beyond posterolateral spines with rounded posterior margin. Coxal spines especially prominent on peraeopods V-VII.

Antenna I short, flagellum only about as long as basal peduncular article; about five groups of aesthetascs on distal half of article. Antenna 2 much shorter than body; three short flagellar articles. Maxilliped with especially long narrow palp; endite only slightly wider than palp with two coupling hooks. Peraeopod I small with no unguis, only long setae on dactylus. Peraeopod II with very short dactylus and unguis. Peraeopods III and IV like I. Peraeopods V-VII each with prominent spine on basis, otherwise normal.

Measurements. Holotype gravid female 9 mm long.

Type locality. Little Nellefiske Bank,

Greenland; Hero 3-29G; 64°54'N, 53°38'W; August 18, 1968; 79-85 m.

Derivation of name. The name 'multispinatus' refers to the many spines on the dorsum of the isopod.

Distribution. Known only from type locality.

Affinities. The species is remarkably like Pleuroprion murdochi (Benedict, 1898) [see Richardson, 1905, p. 342, Figures 371-372], from Point Franklin, Alaska. A deep groove is present in the posterior margin of the pleon in P. murdochi; that of S. multispinatus is rounded. Three coupling hooks are present on the endite of the maxilliped in P. murdochi; two in S. multispinatus. According to the illustrations of Benedict (reproduced also by Richardson), there is a strongly indicated separation between the cephalon and peraeopd I and between pleonal segment 1 and the remainder of the pleon in P. murdochi. Those segments are clearly fused in S. multispinatus. Unfortunately, the peraeopods were not illustrated or described for P. murdochi, so it is not known if they are like those of S. multispinatus.

Remarks. The species was taken at the same location as Arcturus baffini described above.

Rectarcturus gen. nov.

The new genus is composed of four species. One is new, and one is redescribed here. A third and fourth species were formerly in Microarcturus Nordenstam. They are included, although they are slightly different from the new and redescribed species.

Diagnosis. Eyes laterally placed. Body much straighter than in most of arcturids. Cephalon and peraeonal segment I apparently fused. Antenna 2 shorter than body, few flagellar articles. Pleon with no free segments and with small posterolateral spines (more like posterolateral corners).

Description. Eyes large, laterally placed. Short cephalic horns or tubercles present. Dorsum without well-developed spines, but with tubercles and ridges in some species. All appendages short when compared to body length. Edges of peraeonal segments each enlarged with laterally indicated bosses (coxa?) which project beyond anterior border, especially on peraeonal segments II-IV. Antenna 1 compact, only slightly longer than segments 1 and 2 of antenna 2. Each article short, with flagellum only about as long as peduncular segments 2 and 3 combined; few aesthetascs near and at apex. Antenna 2 shorter than body with two to four flagellar articles.

Peraeonal segment V on gravid females abruptly narrower than IV. Pleon compact, anterior indicated segments only barely visible laterally; mediolateral spines absent, only lateral protrusions present. Posterolateral spines short, but definite. Posterior margin produced well beyond posterolateral spines; margin subacutely pointed. Unguis on dactylus of peraeopod I short;

unguis on dactylus of peraeopod II about as long as segment proper. No coupling hooks on endite of maxilliped.

Derivation and gender of name. The name combines the Latin 'rectus' for straight with 'arcturus,' the root of the family name, to indicate the generally straight line formed by the body of specimens of the genus. The gender is masculine.

Type species. Arcturus Kophameli Ohlin, 1901.

Remarks. All specimens known for each species of the genus are gravid females. Microarcturus patagonicus (Ohlin, 1901) is considered to be a member of this genus, and M. Laevis Kensley (1975) should probably be considered to be a member of the genus as well. Microarcturus laevis, according to Kensley's illustration, does have strongly indicated pleonal segments. Both species lack posterior extensions on the posterior margins of peraeonal segments I-III, which are present on the two species described here. Also both have a relatively smooth dorsum. Both, however, have short relatively straight bodies with pleons similar to the shapes of the pleons in the two species described here. Microarcturus laevis, now Rectarcturus laevis (Kensley, 1975), has three flagellar articles on antenna 2 and M. patagonicus has four.

Affinities. The genus is in many ways similar to two other species described as Microarcturus by Kensley: M. similis and M. ornatus, not included because of their dorsal ornamentation and lack of bosses on the edges of the peraeonal segments.

Rectarcturus kophameli (Ohlin)
Figs. 3A-3G

Arcturus Kophameli Ohlin, 1901, p. 272, Figure 5.
Microarcturus kophameli (Ohlin).--Nordenstam, 1933, p. 128

The species is the type of the genus. The redescription here is based on an 8-mm long specimen from the southern tip of South America. It agrees in all details with Ohlin's original description.

Diagnosis. Dorsum with rows of ridges formed of elongated tubercles arranged longitudinally along body. Posterior parts of longitudinal ridges extend beyond posterior main of peraeonal segments especially on segments I-III.

Redescription. Cephalic horns short, between eyes, ridged and folded anteriorly. Deep groove between cephalon and ridged peraeonal segment I. Longitudinal tubercles or ridges on dorsum of peraeonal segments I-VII. Edges of peraeonal segments each enlarged with laterally flat bosses (coxae?) that project beyond anterior border especially on peraeonal segments II-IV. Pleon with anterior three segments hardly indicated; lateral bosses on indicated segment 3; remainder of pleon abruptly lower than anterior part, ending in produced rounded posterior margin. Posterolateral

spines small, angular, and at the end of slight ridges along edge of pleon.

Antenna 1 about 3 times length of basal peduncular segment; flagellum about as long as basal segment, with about six groups of aesthetascs. Antenna 2 about half length of body; two short flagellar articles. Maxilliped normal, with no coupling hooks. Peraeopod I normal. Peraeopod II with proximal three segments short; carpus and propodus each slightly shorter than three proximal segments combined and each with many long setae. Dactylus narrow, elongate and with few setae; unguis narrow, elongate and about as long as dactylus proper. Peraeopods III and IV longer than II, but otherwise similar. Valves smooth.

Measurements. Holotype gravid female 11 mm long.

Type locality. Northern Argentine Basin; 38°S, 50°W, 95 m.

Distribution. The specimen described here was taken much further south of the type locality at two stations near Isla de los Estados--Hero 715-880 and Hero 715-903; 84-208 m.

Material. Each station yielded an 8-mm long gravid female.

Affinities. See R. tuberculatus sp. nov. below.

Rectarcturus tuberculatus sp. nov.
Figs. 4A-4F

Diagnosis. Dorsum tuberculate; some tubercles extend beyond posterior margins on peraeonal segments, especially on I-III.

Description. Cephalic horns short, notched at apexes; folded anteriorly. Cephalon with several small tubercles; tubercles anterior to large tubercles on peraeonal segment I. Many tubercles on all peraeonal segments. Some, especially those on peraeonal segments I-III, extend beyond posterior border of peraeons. Edges of peraeonal segments each, except I, enlarged with laterally flat bosses that project beyond anterior border, especially on peraeonal segments II-IV. Pleon with anterior three segments strongly indicated; edges extended beyond edges of body proper (dorsal view); dorsum with low tubercles. Posterolateral spines moderately large with posterior margin strongly produced and with shallow notch.

Antenna 1 about 3 times length of basal peduncular segment; flagellum about as long as basal segment with about five groups of aesthetascs. Antenna 2 slightly less than half length of body; two flagellar articles. Maxilliped normal with more or less curved sensory edge of endite; exopod with apex broadly rounded. Peraeopod I normal. Peraeopod II with proximal three segments short; carpus and propodus each slightly shorter than three proximal segments combined and each with many long setae. Dactylus narrow, elongate, and with few setae; unguis narrow, elongate, and slightly shorter than dactylus proper. Peraeopods III and IV longer

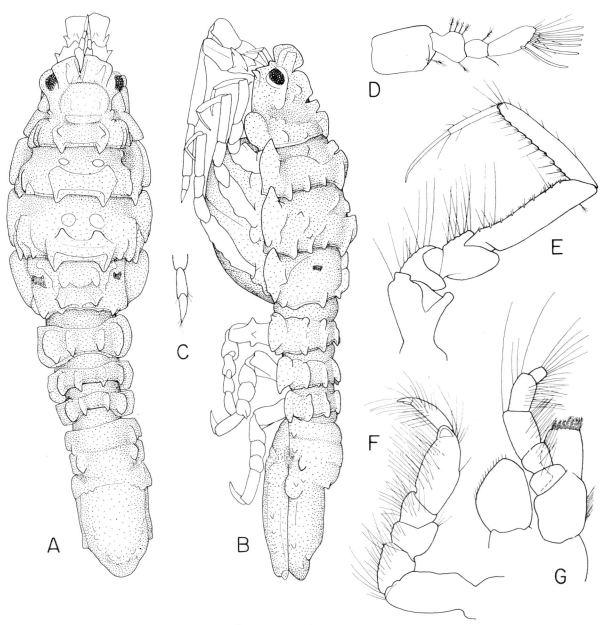

Fig. 3. *Rectarcturus kophameli* (Ohlin, 1901) gen. nov. A, dorsal view gravid female
8 mm long; B, lateral view; C, flagellum antenna 2; D, antenna 1; E, peraeopod II; F,
peraeopod I; G, maxilliped.

than II, with spines on bases especially on IV.
Valves smooth.

Measurements. Holotype gravid female 9.5 mm long.

Derivation of name. The name 'tuberculatus'
refers to the tubercles covering the dorsum.

Type locality. North of South Shetland Islands;
Eltanin 6-363; 57°09'S, 58°58'W; 58°00'S, 58°50'W;
December 7 and 8, 1962; about 3477-3590 m.

Distribution. Known only from type locality.

Affinities. The species is most like the type

species in dorsal ornamentation, having many
rounded tubercles instead of many elongate
ridgelike tubercles. The edges of the peraeons
are similar, and the configuration of the pleons
is similar (especially lateral views).

Remarks. The depth at which this species was
recorded (3477-3560 m) by far exceeds the greatest
depth record (208 m) of the other three species in
the genus. It also is the only one of the four
from south of the Antarctic Convergence.

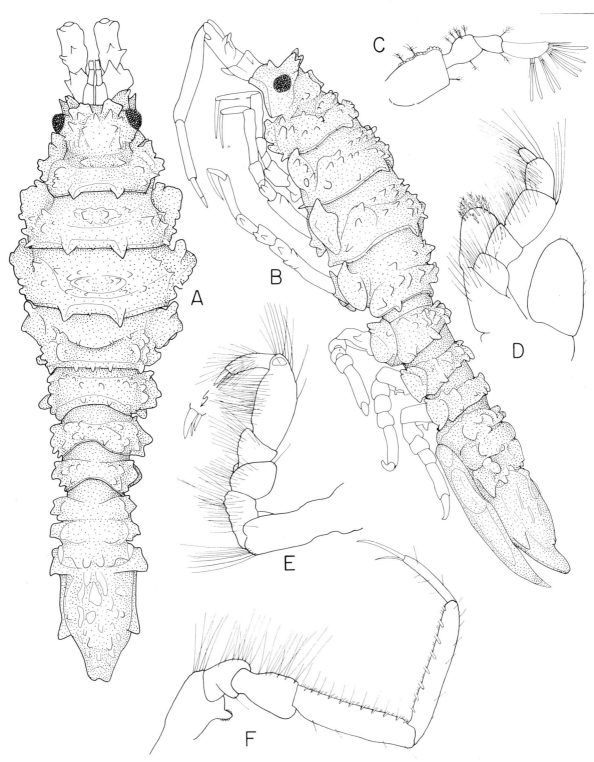

Fig. 4. <u>Rectarcturus</u> <u>tuberculatus</u> gen. nov., sp. nov. A, dorsal view holotype gravid female 9.5 mm long; B, lateral view; C, antenna 1; D, maxilliped; E, peraeopod I; F, peraeopod II.

Rectarcturus patagonicus (Ohlin)

Arcturus patagonicus Ohlin, 1901, p. 271, Figure 4.

Microarcturus patagonicus (Ohlin).--Nordenstam, 1933, p. 128.

The species was obtained near the type locality of, and at the same depth as, R. kophameli (Ohlin). Both species are based on gravid females about 9 mm long.

Diagnosis. Two short cephalic tubercles, not horns, present. Dorsum without strongly indicated tubercles; surface granulate. Posterolateral spines short, but well defined (dorsal view). Body of gravid female narrowest at anterior part of segment V and becomes wider toward pleon.

Measurements. Holotype gravid female 9 mm long.

Type locality. Northern Argentine Basin; 38°S, 56°W; 95 m.

Distribution. Known only from type locality.

Affinities. The shape of the posterior half of the body (see diagnosis) is unique among the species of the genus. The appendages are proportionately longer compared to body length than in other members of the genus. The species also most resembles R. laevis (Kensley, 1975). Both species lack elaborate dorsal ornamentation. Rectarcturus laevis is based on two gravid females (6.4 and 5.2 mm long) from 75 and 48 m deep at False Bay, South Africa. Although the lack of dorsal ornamentation is similar to R. patagonicus, the edges of the peraeonal segments are similar to those of both R. tuberculatus and R. kophameli.

Acantharcturus gen. nov.

Diagnosis. Dorsum of body covered with very long thin spines. Cephalon fused to peraeonal segment I. Pleon with one free segment and posterior margin elongated into a point. Maxilliped endite with one coupling hook.

Derivation and gender of name. The name is from Greek 'akantha' meaning thorn, combined with the root of the family name 'arcturus.' It refers to the dorsal thorns or spines on the body and appendages of the species. The gender is masculine.

Type species. Acantharcturus acutipleon sp. nov.

Affinities. The dorsal ornamentation of long spines is unique among the arcturids.

Acantharcturus acutipleon sp. nov.
Figs. 5A-5K

Diagnosis. See generic diagnosis.

Description. Eyes lateral. Cephalon with two long spines anterior to eyes; five posterior to eyes, one medially placed. Long spines including long medial spine and coxal spines on peraeonal segments I-IV. Segments V-VII and first free and two indicated segments of pleon with long spines but no medial spine. Pleon with long spines on dorsum, ending in strongly produced posterior

margin. Coxae of peraeonal segments V-VII each with long spine.

Antenna 1 with long spine on basal peduncular segment; flagellum longer than three basal segments with about 18 aesthetascs along most of edge. Antenna 2 more than half length of body with several long spines on basal segments; four long flagellar articles. Maxillipedal palp narrow; longer than slightly wider endite; paucuseteous; endite with one coupling hook and one long plumose seta on inner edge; sensory edge with five setae. Peraeopod I with one large spine on basis, ischium, merus, and apex of carpus; few short setae on long dactylus; unguis, long, about one-sixth length of dactylus proper. Valve with row of spines along length. Exopod of male pleopod 1 with produced margin where groove exits.

Measurements. Holotype male 10.6 mm long (including long pleon).

Type locality. West of Antarctic Peninsula nearly on Antarctic Circle; Islas Orcadas 876-122; 61°20.2'S, 44°25.5'W; 61°20.3'S, 44°28.2'W; February 21, 1976; 274.3-285.3 m.

Derivation of name. The species name 'acutipleon' refers to the sharply pointed part of the body.

Distribution. A 10.5-mm long female was also collected slightly west of the type locality. Islas Orcadas 876-118; 274.3-857.7 m.

Affinities. The species is perhaps related to Microarcturus acanthurus (Monod) and M. digitalis Nordenstam. Both have spines that are thicker and shorter than those described here on A. acutipleon. They are also arranged quite differently (i.e., laterally directed) on the posterior peraeonal segments and indicated pleonal segments.

Dolichiscus Richardson

Richardson [1913] instituted the genus on the single species D. pfefferi collected during the Second French Antarctic Expedition. The species has not been recorded since. Antarcturus meridionalis Hodgson, a more commonly encountered species, was suggested to be related by Richardson and formally added to the genus by Tattersall [1921]. As redefined here, Dolichiscus contains seven species (see remarks below), of which two are new. Other workers including Kussakin [1972] and White [1979] do not consider the genus to be valid, but they give no reasons why. The three species of the genus Paradolichiscus gen. nov. described next are also closely related to species of Dolichiscus.

Diagnosis. Body elongate with long spindly appendages. Pleon with one free segment and one very strongly indicated segment. Posterior part of pleon somewhat triangular in cross section with medial dorsal spine above or just before broad posterior border. Posterior border convex or concave. Peraeopod I with dactylus swollen for three quarters of length, abruptly narrowing to support well-defined unguis.

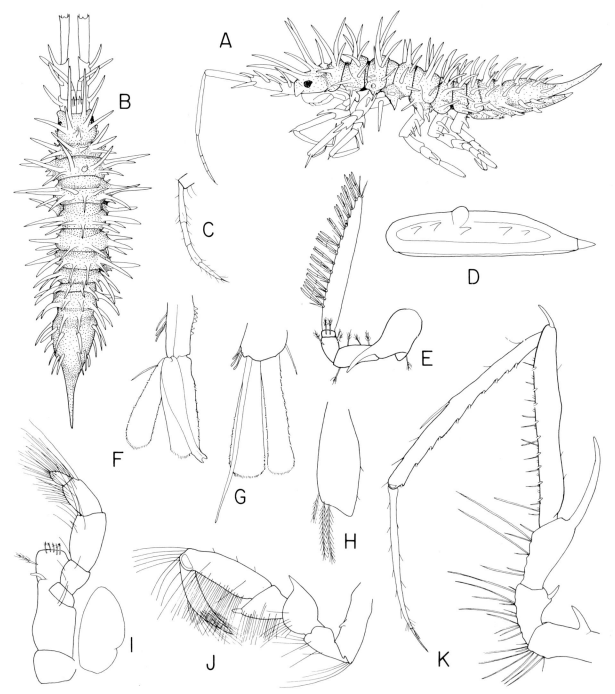

Fig. 5. _Acantharcturus_ _acutipleon_ gen. nov., sp. nov. A, lateral view holotype male
10.6 mm long; B, dorsal view holotype; C, flagellum antenna 2; D, valve; E, antenna 1;
F, G and H, pleopods 1, 2 and 3 male; I, maxilliped; J, peraeopod I; K, peraeopod II.

Description. Eyes lateral, small to large.
Body elongate with long spindly appendages.
Cephalon fused to peraeonal segment I. Dorsum
without dorsal spines; spines, if present, in two
rows along body from cephalon to peraeonal segment
IV on broad-based and laterally indicated segment
and indications of third segment near large
lateral spines. Posterior part of pleon somewhat
triangular in cross section; generally constricted
where attached to peraeon. Medial dorsal spine

above or just before broad posterior border.
Posterior border convex or concave. Many
aesthetascs on long flagellum of antenna 1.
Antenna 2 longer than body with long flagellum of
many articles. Maxilliped with palp normal;
endite without coupling hooks. Peraeopod I small,
gnathal, and with outer margin of dactylus rounded
to form narrow produced distal part, which
supports short or moderately long unguis.
Peraeopod II with inner margin of dactylus with
tiny scales; unguis needlelike and about as long
as dactylus proper. Peraeopods III and IV like
II, but longer. Peraeopods V-VII long and
spindly. Valve smooth, with small tubercles or
with small spines.

Derivation and gender of name. The name is from
the Greek 'dolichos' meaning long, with the
diminutive suffix 'iscus,' which apparently means
'a little long,' perhaps referring to the lengthy
body and appendages of the type species. The
gender, not indicated by Richardson, is here
considered to be masculine.

Type species. Dolichiscus pfefferi Richardson,
1913; type by monotypy.

Affinities. The genus is related to
Paradolichiscus gen nov. described below.

Remarks. The species in the genus are D.
pfefferi Richardson, 1913; D. meridionalis
(Hodgson, 1910); D. profundus sp. nov.; D.
acanthaspidus sp. nov.; D. anna (Beddard, 1886),
and D. diana sp. nov. In addition to these
species, which are described or diagnosed here,
Arcurus cornutus Beddard (1886, p. 93, Plate 19,
figs. 6-12) from southeast of the Phillipine
Islands (Challenger station 214; 914.4 m) should
be included in Dolichiscus. Dolichiscus pfefferi,
D. meridionalis, and D. profundus sp. nov. are
closely related to each other. Less closely
related is D. acanthaspidus sp. nov. Dolichiscus
anna; D. diana sp. nov., and D. cornutus are also
more closely related to each other than to the
other four. Species of Paradolichiscus gen. nov.,
described below, are related, but even less so, to
the seven species of Dolichiscus.

Dolichiscus pfefferi Richardson

Dolichiscus pfefferi Richardson, 1913, p. 14,
    Figure 2.--Tattersall, 1921, p. 243.--Nordenstam,
    1933, p. 127.--Hale, 1946, p. 197.

The species is the type of the genus.
Diagnosis. Pleon more than one-third length of
body, expanded posteriorly and ending in single
large, medial, posterior spine situated above
broad posterior border. Many more than 19
flagellar articles on antenna 2. Lateral margins
of peraeonal segments I-IV expanded, produced, and
ending in acute points.

Type locality. Marguerite Bay; 67°43'S,
70°45'45"W; January 15, 1909; 254 m.

Affinities. The species is most nearly like D.
meridionalis and D. profundus sp. nov. It differs
from these two in that the edges of peraeonal

segments I-IV are expanded and pointed.

Remarks. The species is not a form of the adult
female of D. meridionalis as has been suggested by
Tattersall [1921]. Hale [1946] and Kussakin
[1967, p. 299] considered it to be a valid
species, but Kussakin [1972, p. 178] did not
consider the genus to be valid.

Dolichiscus meridionalis (Hodgson)
Figs. 6A-6G and 7A-7C.

Antarcturus meridionalis Hodgson, 1910, p. 43,
    Plate 6, fig. 2.
Dolichiscus meridionalis (Hodgson).--Richardson,
    1913, p. 17.--Tattersall, 1921, p. 243.--Hale,
    1946, p. 197, Figure 22.--Kussakin, 1967, p. 298.

The species is circum-Antarctic in distribution
and was encountered by three other workers after
it was described.

Diagnosis. Dorsum relatively smooth. Pleon
over one-third length of body, expanded
posteriorly and ending in single medial dorsal
spine situated above concave posterior border.
Only margin of peraeonal segment I extended
laterally. Antenna 2 much longer than length of
body; long flagellum of many thin articles. Eight
spines on inner margin of carpus of peraeopod VII
of male.

Redescription. Eyes lateral. Body smooth,
elongate; appendages long, especially antenna 2,
pleon about two-fifths length of body. Cephalon
and peraeonal segment I fused; segment I with wide
spinelike lateral projection. Pleon long and with segment
(especially anterior part), long and with segment
1 indicated and segment 2 partially indicated; no
lateral spines on indicated segment 3; posterior
border convex. Coxae without spines. Antenna 1
with flagellum longer than three peduncular
segments combined; about 18 groups of aesthetascs
along most of edge. Antenna 2 thin, much longer
than twice body length; flagellum (no unbroken
flagella were found) multiarticulate (27+ articles
long); flagellum longer than each peduncular
segment and about as long as body (even broken).
Maxilliped with palp longer than endite; sensory
edge with many specialized setae. Exopod of
maxilliped subtriangular. Peraeopod I small,
gnathal, with outer edge of dactylus rounded;
distal part produced supporting small unguis.
Peraeopod II with needlelike unguis on dactylus;
unguis slightly longer than dactylus proper; inner
margin of dactylus minutely scaled. Peraeopods
III and IV like II, but longer. Peraeopods V-VII
long and spindly with each segment elongate.
Carpus of peraeopod VII with six spines on convex
inner margin. Penis elongate. Valve smooth.

Measurements. Males to 43 mm, gravid females to
48 mm long. Specimens from this collection (24)
include males to 36 mm and gravid females to 43 mm
long.

Type locality. Ross Sea off Great Ice Barrier;
January 27, 1902; 549 m.

Distribution. Circum-Antarctic, 24-2000 m.

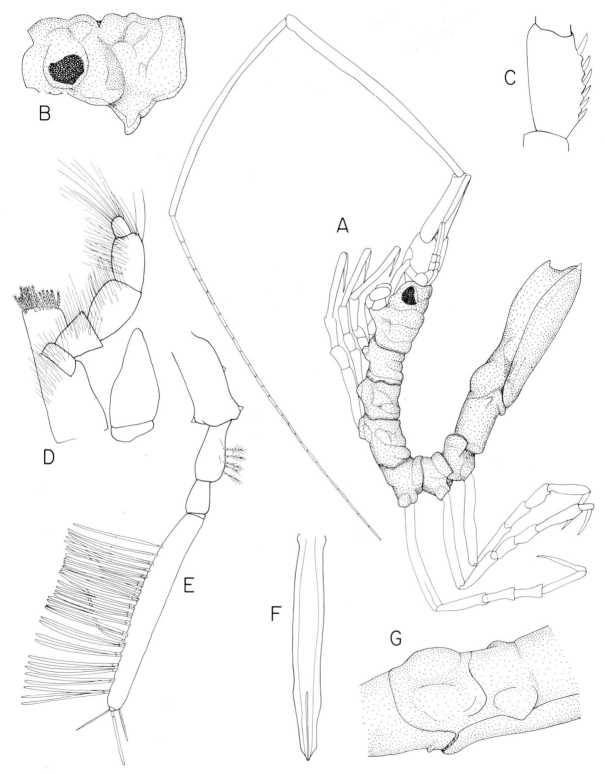

Fig. 6. <u>Dolichiscus meridionalis</u> (Hodgson, 1910). A, male 32 mm long; B, oblique view cephalon and peraeonal segment I; C, carpus male peraeopod VI; D, maxilliped; E, antenna 1; F, penis; G, oblique view anterior part of pleon.

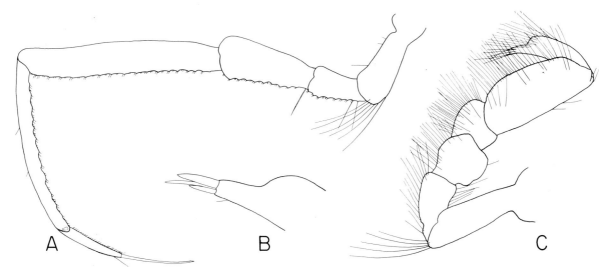

Fig. 7. Dolichiscus meridionalis (Hodgson, 1910). A, peraeopod I; B, distal part
dactylus peraeopod I; C, peraeopod I.

Material. Eltanin 51-5762 (one female 33 mm),
Eltanin 12-1082 (one male 29 mm, one female 28
mm), Eltanin 22-1521 (one immature 10 mm), Eltanin
27-1892 (one male 36 mm), Eltanin 27-1930 (one
female 35 mm), Eltanin 32-2050 (one male 32 mm,
two females 33 and 42 mm), Eltanin 32-2034 (one
male 31 mm), Eltanin 32-2065 (one male 36 mm, one
female 41 mm), Eltanin 32-2082 (one female 43 mm),
Eltanin 32-2088 (one female 35 mm), Eltanin
51-5761 (one immature 13 mm), Eltanin 51-5762 (one
male 33 mm, one female 33 mm, three fragments),
Eltanin 51-5765 (one female 33 mm), Hero 721-726
(one female 30 mm), Hero 721-776 (one female 41
mm), and Islas Orcadas 876-107 (one female 37
mm). Twenty-four specimens--six males, thirteen
females, two immature, and three fragments.

Affinities. The species is most like D.
profundus, which has smaller eyes and fewer spines
(3) on the carpus of peraeopod VI of the male. It
is also like D. pfefferi, but lacks the expansions
on the edges of peraeonal segment I-IV, which are
characteristic of that species.

Remarks. The station Eltanin 51-5762 yielded
both D. meridionalis and D. acanthaspidius.

Dolichiscus profundus sp. nov.
Figs. 8A-8J

Diagnosis. Eyes small. Lateral spines on
peraeonal segment I short. Three spines on inner
margin of carpus of peraeopod VI of the male.

Description. Eyes small and lateral. Body
smooth; appendages long; pleon about two-fifths
body length. Cephalon and peraeonal segment I
fused; segment I with very short lateral
extensions. Pleonal segment 1 indicated; segment
2 partially indicated; short lateral spines on
indicated segment 3; posterior border convex.
Coxae with tiny spines. Antenna 1 with flagellum

about 2 times length of three peduncular segments
combined; about 56 groups of aesthetascs along
entire length of flagellum. Antenna 2 longer than
body; flagellum with long articles (broken).
Maxilliped with palp much longer than endite;
exopod subtriangular. Peraeopod I short, gnathal
with outer edge of dactylus rounded; distal part
produced supporting small unguis. Peraeopod with
needlelike unguis on dactylus; unguis longer than
dactylus proper; inner margin of dactylus minutely
scaled. Peraeopods III and IV like II, but
longer. Carpus of peraeopod VI with three spines
on convex inner margin. Penis elongate. Valves
minutely tuberculated.

Measurements. Holotype male 37 mm long.

Type locality. About 275 km east of Cape
Hallett; Eltanin 32-2113; 73°19'S, 174°53'W;
73°19'S, 174°52'W; February 9, 1968; 2897-2907 m.

Derivation of name. The name 'profundus,' from
Latin for deep, refers to the depth of the type
locality, which is greater than for D.
meridionalis, the more common species.

Distribution. Known only from type locality.

Affinities. The species is most like D.
meridionalis, but it has smaller eyes and three
instead of six spines on the inner margin of the
carpus of peraeopod VI. The lateral spines on
peraeonal segment I are small, not greatly
developed as they are on D. meridionalis or on D.
pfefferi. The pleon is proportionately thicker,
especially where it attaches to the peraeon. Also
pleonal segment 1 is much shorter in D. profundus.

Remarks. Assuming that the other species of the
genus have eyes of normal size, the eyes in this
species are small, perhaps reflecting the great
depth (about 2900 m) at which it was collected.
It seems to be a species that evolved in the
deeper habitat from D. meridionalis (greatest
depth about 2000 m).

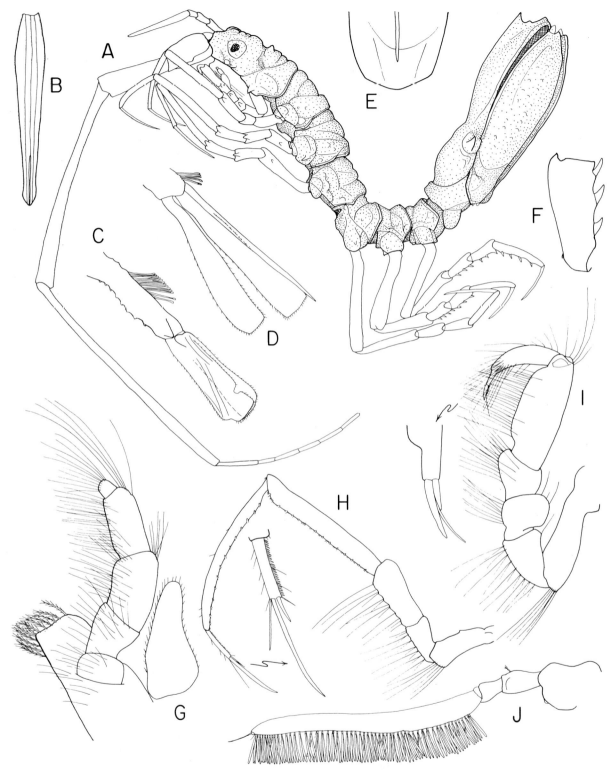

Fig. 8. _Dolichiscus profundus_ sp. nov. A, holotype male 37 mm long; B, penis; C,
pleopod 1; D, pleopod 2; E, dorsal view posterior margin pleon; F, carpus peraeopod
VI; C, maxilliped; H, peraeopod II; I, peraeopod I; J, antenna 1.

Dolichiscus acanthaspidius sp. nov.
Figs. 9A-9I

The species is the only one in the genus with many hairlike setae on the spines and body.

Diagnosis. Dorsum of cephalon and peraeonal segments I-V each with four long spines. Appendages and spines with many long hairlike setae. Large setae-bearing spines project ventrolaterally from anterior part of pleon just anterior to valves.

Description. Eyes lateral. Body surface granulate with long hairlike setae on spines and on margins of pleon and valves. Antenna 2 and peraeopods densely covered with setae. Cephalon and peraeonal segment I fused; segments I-IV each with four long dorsal spines bearing setae (especially in larger individuals). Two short dorsal spines on peraeonal segments V-VII and three pleonal segments in larger individuals. Pleon with one free and one strongly indicated segment; pleon elongate with one medial dorsal spine above and slightly anterior to posterior rounded margin. Lateral spines on indicated pleonal segment 3 with hairlike setae on them. Anterior part of pleon with four long ventrally projecting spines each bearing hairlike setae. Coxae with long spines. Antenna 1 with large basis and with four long spines; flagellum slightly shorter than three peduncular segments combined; about nine groups of aesthetascs along slightly more than half length of flagellum. Antenna 2 longer than body; flagellum (paratype) about as long as distal most two peduncular segments of flagellum; 12 flagellar articles. Maxilliped with narrow palp; sensory edge with many special setae; exopod with acutely pointed apex. Peraeopod I elongate with normal dactylus. Peraeopod II with long spines on proximal segments; dactylus about half as long as needlelike unguis. Peraeopods III and IV longer than II with long spines on proximal segments, otherwise similar to peraeopod II. Peraeopods V-VII elongate with bases minutely tuberculate. Valves smooth.

Measurements. Holotype female 33 mm long, male 27 mm long.

Type locality. About 175 km east of Cape Hallett; Eltanin 51-5762; 76°2.07'S, 179°56.98'W; 76°2.30'S, 179°52.14'W; 347-358 m.

Derivation of name. The Greek words 'acantha' (thorn) and 'aspidos' (shield) are combined to mean 'a thorny shield' and refer to the dorsal spines on the anterior part of the body.

Distribution. Outer part of Ross Sea and near Balleny Islands; 55-622 m.

Material. Eltanin 27-1885 (one male 25 mm), Eltanin 27-1877 (one male 27 mm), Eltanin 32-2123 (one female 31 mm), Eltanin 32-2124 (one female 30 mm) and Balleny Islands (one immature 11 mm). Five specimens--two males, two females, and one immature.

Remarks. Larger individuals tend to have more hairlike setae than smaller individuals. Also they tend to have two small dorsal spines on peraeonal segments V-VII and on the anterior three segments of the pleon, which continues the two rows of spines along the whole body. Station Eltanin 51-5762 yielded both D. acanthaspidius and D. meridionalis.

Affinities. The species is most like D. meridionalis, but it has dorsal spines on the anterior part of the body. Antenna 2 is proportionately much shorter, and the flagellum is short and with fewer articles in D. acanthaspidius.

Dolichiscus anna (Beddard)

Arcturus anna Beddard, 1886, p. 91, Plate 19, figs. 1-5.
Antarcturus anna (Beddard).--Nordenstam, 1933, p. 128.--Kussakin, 1967, p. 291.

Specimens were taken, but not illustrated or described, by Kussakin [1967] from near the type locality.

Diagnosis. Dorsal spines absent; coxal and other lateral spines well developed. Pleon with long lateral spines on indicated segment 3; small mediolateral spines; posterolateral edges of pleon produced as broad-based long spines.

Measurements. Holotype female 37 mm long. Gravid female 53 mm long [Kussakin, 1967].

Type locality. Off Río de la Plata, Argentine Basin; Challenger station 320; 37°17'S, 53°52'W; February 14, 1876; 1097 m.

Distribution. Argentine Basin. Type locality and Ob station 480 nearby; 399-1097 m.

Affinities. The species is very closely related to D. diana sp. nov. (see under that species). It is also related to D. cornutus (Beddard) from southeast of the Philippine Islands.

Dolichiscus diana sp. nov.
Figs. 10A-10D and 11A-11B

The new species from south of the Antarctic Convergence is much like D. anna (Beddard) from the Argentine Basin, but it has more spines on its body.

Diagnosis. Eyes lateral and very large. Laterally projecting spines well developed on peraeonal and pleonal segments. Cephalon and peraeonal segment I fused; pleon with segment 1 free and 2 strongly indicated; indicated segment 3 with long spines.

Description. Eyes lateral and very large. Cephalon and peraeonal segment I fused. Cephalon with four small dorsal tubercles. Peraeonal segments I-IV with small laterally projecting spines; lateral margins with long laterally projecting acutely pointed expansions. Peraeonal segments V-VII with laterally projecting spines on indicated peraeonal segment 3. Dorsum of pleon and valves with small scalelike tubercles on surfaces. Six long spines ventrally located anterior to valves.

Antenna 1 with very small basal peduncular

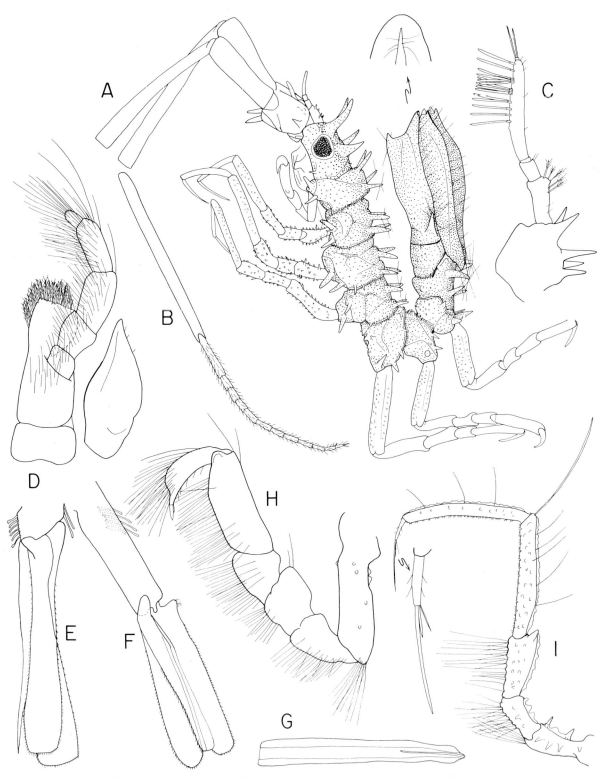

Fig. 9. <u>Dolichiscus acanthaspidius</u> sp. nov. A, holotype female 33 mm long; B, antenna 2 (paratype); C, antenna 1; D, maxilliped; E, pleopod 2 male 27 mm long; F, pleopod 1 male; G, penis; H, female peraeopod I; I, female peraeopod II.

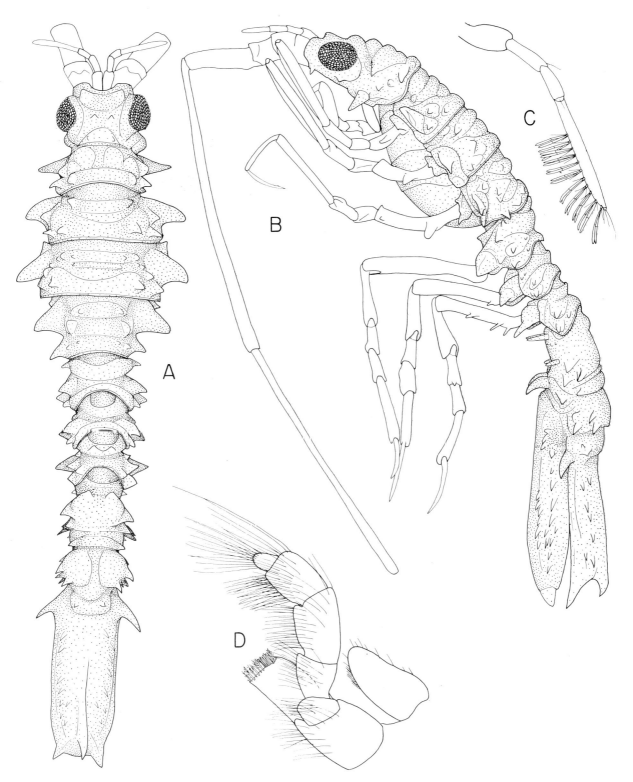

Fig. 10. Dolichiscus diana sp. nov. A, holotype gravid female 23 mm long; B, lateral view holotype female; C, antenna 1; D, maxilliped.

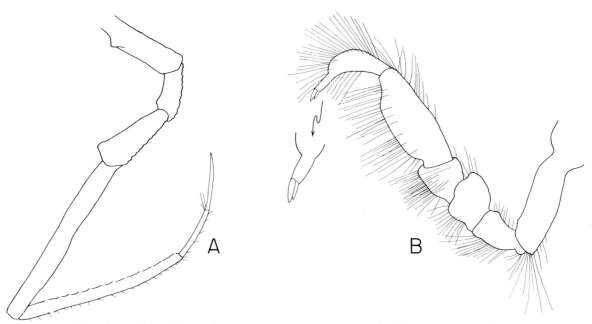

Fig. 11. *Dolichiscus diana* sp. nov. A, peraeopod II; B, peraeopod I.

segment subequal in length to peduncular segments 2 and 3 combined; flagellum about as long as three peduncular segments combined; about 11 groups of aesthetascs. Antenna 2 longer than body; flagellum missing. Maxilliped with palp longer than endite; exopod small with rounded apex. Peraeopod I elongate and normal. Peraeopod II with small spine on basis; dactylus elongate, unguis about as long as basis proper. Peraeopods III-IV with long spines on basis, longer than peraeonal segment II; unguis about as long as dactylus. Valve with small scalelike tubercles.

Measurements. Holotype gravid female 23 mm long.

Type locality. Just north of South Georgia; Islas Orcadas 876-122; 60°26.5'S, 46°22.8'W; 60°26.5'S, 46°22.8'W; February 16, 1976; 274-285.

Derivation of name. The name, from Diana, goddess of the chase, is related to the 'anna' of Beddard.

Distribution. Known only from type locality.

Affinities. The laterally projecting spines on the peraeon and anterior part of the pleon are more numerous and better developed in D. diana than in D. anna. Small spines are present on the dorsum of the pleon and on the valves on D. diana. They are absent in D. anna. The two species are closely related to C. cornutus, which has long cephalic horns and more elongate, sharper spines laterally placed than in either of the two species.

Paradolichiscus gen. nov.

The genus is composed of one new and two other species. All are from south of the Antarctic Convergence. They resemble species of Dolichiscus, but are covered with short or long dorsal and coxal spines.

Diagnosis. Eyes small. Cephalon and peraeonal segment I fused. Body covered with short or long spines. Pleon with one free segment. Posterior margin of pleon with one short or long medial spine. Appendages long and spindly with many spines, especially on proximal part of segments. Peraeopod I with outer margin of dactylus rounded subapically; distal part of dactylus produced supporting short unguis.

Description. Eyes small. Body and appendages long and spindly. Body covered with short or long spines. Cephalon and peraeonal segment I fused. Pleon with one free segment; segment 2 strongly indicated; long lateral spines on indicated segment 3. Pleon over one-third length of body. Large or small medial spine dorsally placed on posterior part of pleon. Coxae with long spines. Antenna 1 with long spine on relatively small basal segment; flagellum elongate with many groups of aesthetascs. Antenna 2 longer than body; flagellum long and multiarticulate. Peraeopod I with outer margin of dactylus rounded subapically; distal part of dactylus produced supporting short unguis. Peraeopod II with many long setae on carpus and propodus; dactylus short, thin, and with unguis much longer than dactylus proper. All peraeopods with long spines on proximal segments. Peraeopods III and IV longer than II. Peraeopods V-VII long and spindly; carpus on VII sometimes modified (sexually dimorphic?). Valves covered with long spines.

Derivation and gender of name. The prefix 'para' is from the Greek, meaning near. The new genus is related to or near Dolichiscus

Richardson, the second part of the name. The gender is masculine.

Type species. Antarcturus gaussianus Vanhöffen, 1914. Type because it is the oldest described species in the genus.

Affinities. The species of the genus are most like those in Dolichiscus. Species of Paradolichiscus, however, have long or short spines on the dorsum. One free and one strongly indicated segment are present on the pleon. The eyes are small in species of Paradolichiscus and of moderate or large size in species of Dolichiscus. The general shape of the body, the long spindly appendages, and the individual shapes of each appendage are characters common to members of both genera.

Paradolichiscus gaussianus (Vanhöffen)
Figs. 12A-12E

Antarcturus gaussianus Vanhöffen, 1914, p. 520, Figures 52A-52C.

The species is the type of the genus. The redescription and illustrations are based on a 33-mm long female from just north of the Ross Sea.

Diagnosis. Appendages greatly elongate. Pleon and uropods covered with long, large spines. Single very large medial spine projecting over more or less truncate posterior margin of pleon.

Redescription. Eyes small. Cephalon and fused peraeonal segment I with few short dorsal spines. Peraeonal segments II-IV with short spines on dorsum. Pleon with elongate thin free segment 1 with four ventrally directed spines. Elongate pointed lateral spines on indicated segment 3. Many large spines on indicated segment 3. Many large spines on dorsum of pleon and on valves. Medial dorsal spine particularly large, extending beyond posterior margin of pleon. Coxae with long spines.

Antenna 1 with long spine on basal segment; flagellum longer than three peduncular segments combined, with about 18 groups of aesthetascs spread over about two-thirds length of flagellum. Antenna 2 broken. Maxilliped with long palp, apical article small; exopod subtriangular. Peraeopod I normal. Peraeopod II both broken; dactylus with long unguis combined shorter than propodus on peraeopod IV. Peraeopods in general long, but stout; basal segments with many long spines. Valves with very long spines (somewhat damaged).

Measurements. Holotype female 34 mm long.

Type locality. Off Wilhelm II Coast; Gauss station near 90°E; March 1, 1903; 2450 m.

Distribution. East Antarctic and north of Ross Sea; 2450-3492 m. A 33-mm long female was collected at Eltanin 27-1859.

Affinities. The species is much like Paradolichiscus debilis and P. opiliones sp. nov. Both have shorter and smaller spines on the pleon than those present on P. gaussianus.

Remarks. The specimens as illustrated by

Vanhöffen [1914] have longer spines on the cephalon and peraeonal segments when compared to the specimen illustrated here. A parasitic species of cryptoniscid of the genus Arcturocheres Hansen [1916] was living attached to the marsupium of the 33-mm long female specimen [Schultz, 1980].

Paradolichiscus debilis (Hale)

Antarcturus debilis Hale, 1937, p. 27, Figures 8 and 9.

The species was caught at the most shallow location (526 m) of the three species of the genus included here.

Diagnosis. Body surface smooth, but with many small spines. Posterior margin of pleon truncate slightly produced medially below small medial spine. Small spine at each corner of posterior border of pleon. Ventral margin of peraeonal segment I straight and without spines.

Description. The species was adequately described and illustrated by Hale [1937].

Measurements. Holotype male 25 mm long.

Type locality. Off George V Coast; Australasian Antarctic Expedition 1914; station ii; 66°55'S, 145°21'E; 526-549 m.

Affinities. The species is much like Paradolichiscus opiliones sp. nov. (see under that species).

Paradolichiscus opiliones sp. nov.
Figs. 13A-13I

The species was taken at a depth greater than any species of Arcturidae described here (4187-4209 m).

Diagnosis. Body red with moderately long spines. Peraeopods especially long and spindly. Carpus of peraeopod VI of male modified with two lobes, each of which is topped with large setae. Ventral main of peraeonal segment I with large spines.

Description. Eyes small. Cephalon with horns and other spines; peraeonal segment I with many moderately long dorsal, lateral, and ventral spines. Peraeonal segments II-VII all with long spines on dorsum. Dorsum of pleon and valves with long spines. Free segments of pleon narrow with ventral spines and long ventrolateral spines. Lateral spines on indicated segment 3 short but distinct. Posterior margin of pleon broadly rounded with one medial and two posterolateral spines projecting beyond it. Coxae with long setae.

Antenna 1 with one spine on proportionately small basal segment; peduncular segments 2 and 3 long; flagellum longer than three peduncular segments combined, with about 40 groups of aesthetascs covering over three-quarters length of flagellum. Antenna 2 longer than body; flagellum broken. Maxilliped with elongate palp, distal article small; many setae on sensory edge; exopod small and subtriangular. Peraeopod I elongate;

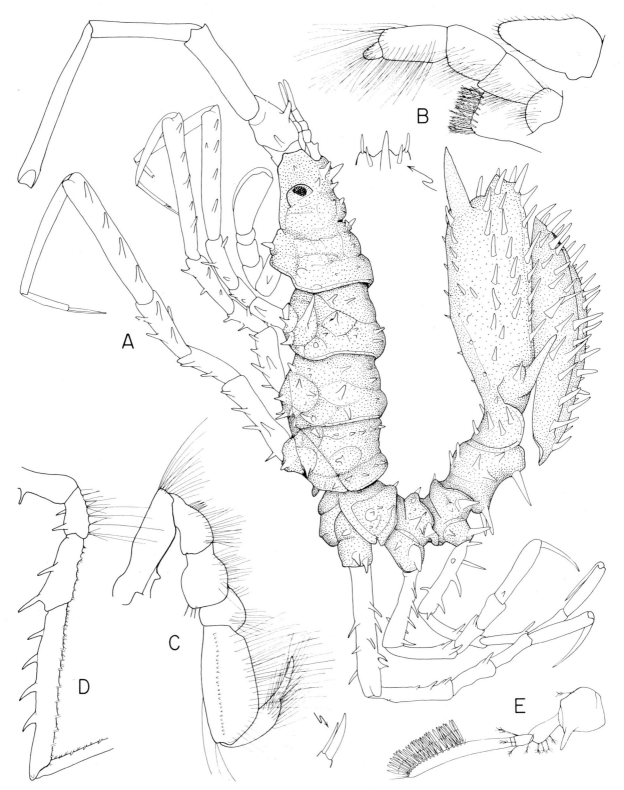

Fig. 12. _Paradolichiscus gaussianus_ (Vanhöffen, 1914) gen. nov. A, gravid female 28 mm long; B, maxilliped; C, peraeopod I; D, peraeopod II; E, antenna 1.

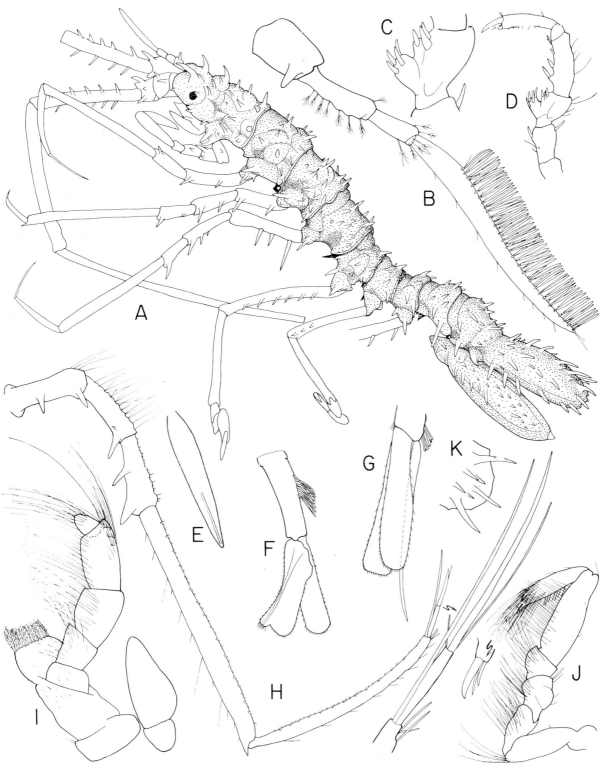

Fig. 13. _Paradolichiscus_ _opiliones_ gen. nov., sp. nov. A, holotype male 35 mm long; B, antenna 1; C, detail carpus peraeopod VI male; D, peraeopod VI; E, penis; F, pleopod 1; G, pleopod 2; H, peraeopod II; I, maxilliped; J, peraeopod I; dorsal view posterior margin pleon.

dactylus normal. Peraeopod II elongate, especially carpus and propodus; dactylus very short with unguis more than twice as long as propodus. Penis long, tapering to point distally. Outer margin of pleopod 1 of male produced where groove leaves. Valve with large spines.

Measurements. Holotype male 33 mm long.

Type locality. About 2500 km southeast of New Zealand; Eltanin 14-1192; 55°55'S, 159°52'W; 54°47'S, 159°50'W; August 6, 1964, 4187-4209 m.

Derivation of name. The species name 'opiliones' is the name of the group of harvestman (daddy-long-leg) spiders, which this species with its long legs resembles.

Distribution. Known only from type locality.

Affinities. The species is most like P. debilis, but that species has much smaller spines on the dorsum. Unfortunately, only a female was described for P. debilis, so the significance of the particular configuration of the carpus of the male for identification remains to be seen.

Caecarcturus gen. nov.

The genus contains a blind species which is unique among the arcturids from Antarctica. The pattern of the spines is also unique.

Diagnosis. Blind. Cephalon and peraeonal segment I fused; body with small tubercles. Four long horizontally directed spines, one pair on peraeonal segment I and one pair on peraeonal segment III. Pleon with three indicated segments; segment 3 with laterally directed spines; posterolateral spines absent; posterior margin pointed.

Derivation and gender of name. The name is from the Latin 'caecus,' meaning blind, and 'arcturus,' the root of the family name. It means blind arcturid. The gender is masculine.

Type species. Caecarcturus quadraspinosus sp. nov.

Caecarcturus quadraspinosus sp. nov.
Figs. 14A-14K

Small rounded tubercles without signs of ocelli or pigment are present where the eyes should be.

Diagnosis. See generic diagnosis.

Description. Blind; small rounded tubercles without any sign of ocelli or pigment present laterally on cephalon. No spines or tubercles dorsally placed. Deep groove between fused cephalon and peraeonal segment I. Peraeonal segments II and IV-VII with only groups of small tubercles on rounded side. Pleon short with fused segments; indicated segment 3 with large lateral spines; posterolateral corners absent; posterior margin acutely pointed. Coxae small without spines.

Antenna 1 elongate; basal peduncular segment short and only slightly wider than other segments; segment 2 elongate; segments 3 shorter than 1; flagellum longer than three combined peduncular

segments with about 13 groups of aesthetascs along about two thirds of margin. Antenna 2 longer than body with most distal peduncular segment longest and longer than flagellum; flagellum thin with four articles.

Maxilliped with palp longer than endite; apical two articles much narrower than proximal three articles; inner margin of articles 3 and 4 convex; exopod diamond shaped. Peraeopod I with short unguis on normal dactylus; carpus and merus with toothlike setae on inner margin. Peraeopod II with toothlike setae on inner margin of four proximal segments; length of dactylus minus unguis almost same as length of propodus; inner margin with very large spinelike setae; unguis slightly less than half length of dactylus proper; second apical claw about as large as unguis proper. Valve smooth, tapering to point posteriorly.

Measurements. Holotype female 4.5 mm long.

Type locality. East of Bounty and Antipodes Island off New Zealand; Eltanin 27-1851; 49°40'S, 178°53'W; 49°40'S, 178°54'W; January 3, 1957; 439-540 m.

Derivation of name. The species name 'quadraspinosus' refers to the four long laterally projecting spines on the body of the specimen.

Distribution. Known only from type locality.

Affinities. The species is unique among arcturids from Antarctica in being blind and in its particular pattern of spination on the peraeon.

Remarks. A small blind immature paratype 3.5 mm long (Figure 14K) looks more like the typical arcturid. It has short dorsal tubercles, which will grow into the four long spines of the adult. The pleon is pointed and shaped much like that of the adult.

Cylindrarcturus gen. nov.

Diagnosis. Eyes large and laterally placed. Elongate smooth body; pointed pleon over one-third length of body. Antenna 2 shorter than length of body. Segment IV only slightly longer than other peraeonal segments. Pleon long and pointed.

Derivation and gender of name. The name refers to the cylindrical nature of the body, added to the root of the family name 'arcturus.' The gender is masculine.

Affinities. The smooth, thin body suggests that the genus be placed near the Astacilla genera of the family, but the short peraeonal segment IV makes it more like the Arcturus members of the family.

Cylindrarcturus elongatus sp. nov.
Figs. 15A-15J

Diagnosis. See generic diagnosis.

Description. Eyes very large and laterally placed. Body smooth without spines. Cephalon and peraeonal segments fused. Peraeonal segment IV not noticeably longer than other peraeonal segments. Pleon with segments indicated, cylindrical, elongate posterior margin produced to

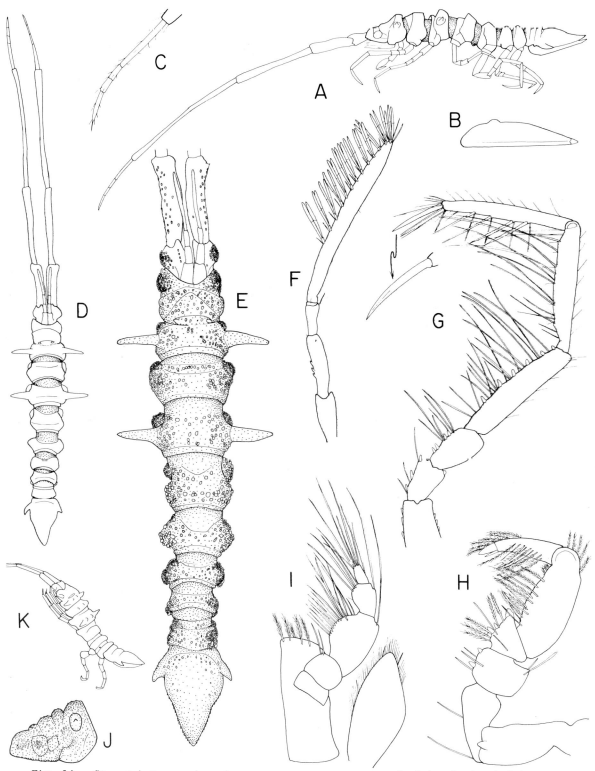

Fig. 14. Caecarcturus quadraspinosus gen. nov., sp. nov. A, lateral view holotype female 7.5 mm long; B, valve; C, flagellum antenna 2; D, dorsal view holotype; E, enlarged dorsal view; F, antenna 1; G, peraeopod II; H, peraeopod I; I, maxilliped; J, lateral view cephalon-peraeonal segment I; K, immature 3.5 mm long.

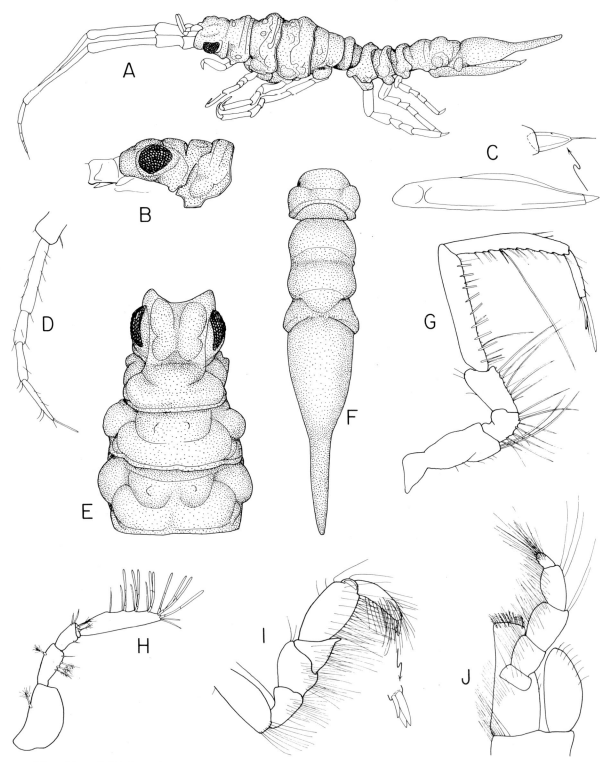

Fig. 15. <u>Cylindrarcturus elongatus</u> gen. nov., sp. nov. A, holotype female 12.4 mm long; B, lateral view cephalon and peraeopod II; C, valve; D, detail flagellum antenna 2; E, dorsal view cephalon and peraeonal segments I-III; F, dorsal view posterior part of peraeon and pleon; G, peraeopod II; H, antenna 1; I, peraeopod I; J, maxilliped.

long acutely ending point. Antenna 1 with flagellum shorter than three peduncular segments; about seven aesthetacs on over half of margin. Antenna 2 shorter than length of body; four long flagellar articles. Maxilliped with palp slightly longer than endite; sensory edge with many setae; exopod with rounded apical margin. Peraeopod I short, gnathal, and with short unguis on normal dactylus. Peraeopod II with basis about as long as ischium and merus combined; carpus and propodus each less in length than combined basal segments; dactylus proper short, about as long as merus and supporting slightly longer unguis. Valve smooth.

Measurements. Holotype gravid female 12.4 mm long.

Type locality. Anvers Island region; Hero 721-726; 62°19.3'S, 59°11.8'W; 62°19.2'S, 59°11.7'W; December 26, 1971; 64-89 m.

Derivation of name. The species name 'elongatus' refers to the elongate body, especially the pleon with its long posterior margin.

Distribution known only from type locality.

Affinities. The presence of an unguis on the dactylus of peraeopod I suggests that the species is more related to the Arcturus-like members of the genus rather than the Astacilla-like members, as the general body shape suggests.

Astacilla Cordiner

The genus was described by Cordiner [1795] and has been a broadly defined genus, where many species have been placed by many workers. It is still not rigidly defined, and no attempt is made here to do so. The two species formerly in Neastacilla Tattersall [1921] from the Antarctic region are included here under Astacilla. Although Nordenstam [1933, p. 119] used Neastacilla to contain N. kerguelensis Vanhöffen, he stated that the genus might be 'superfluous,' hence a junior synonym of Astacilla. Hale [1946], who described what would have been Neastacilla kerguelensis from Île Kerguelen, kept it in Astacilla and abolished the genus by stating that the only criterion by which he could define Neastacilla was that one seta in the fringing setae on the dactylus of peraeopod I in N. kerguelensis might be regarded as a particular elongate claw; hence it might really be the unguis of the dactylus. Since this is a superficial distinction and based only on interpretation, the genus Neastacilla Tattersall is not regarded as valid here and the two species from the Antarctic region, N. falclandica and N. magellanica, are placed in Astacilla. Since N. falclandica is the type species of the genus and it was designated so by Tattersall, the genus is no longer valid.

The species are then placed in Astacilla, which itself is not well defined, having once been, with Arcturus, one of the only two genera in the family. Astacilla contains many species, only a few of which are well defined. The characters that set the species apart from one another and the characters that are used to define other closely related genera are not always as distinct as they might be, so considerable work must be done to redefine the genus proper.

Here a diagnosis of the genus is given, which is essentially based on species from the Antarctic region. It is important to remember that it is brief and most probably does not apply to all species recorded in the genus at present.

Diagnosis. Eyes present. Dorsum with little or no dorsal ornamentation. Cephalon and peraeonal segment I with deep furrow between. Peraeonal segment I with or without pleura elongated ventrally. Peraeonal segment IV much longer than cephalon and peraeonal segments I-III combined. Peraeopods I-IV short with long hairlike setae on distal segments; peraeopods folded forward ventrally under cephalon; peraeopods V-VII short and prehensile. Pleon with three usually only indicated segments; usually only bumps laterally placed on indicated segment 3; posterolateral spines tiny or absent; posterior margin usually produced into elongate point. Antenna 2 usually shorter than body; flagellum with few articles sometimes clawlike. Peraeopod I short, gnathal, and with short dactylus fringed with long setae. Valves usually smooth.

Derivation and gender of name. The name is from the Greek 'astakos,' meaning lobster or crayfish, which with the diminutive suffix added means small lobster or crayfish. The gender is feminine.

Type species. Oniscus longicornis Sowerby, 1806 (see Gruner [1965]). The species apparently was chosen by Cordiner [1975] to form the genus; hence it is the type species because it was the first species placed in the genus.

Remarks. Kussakin [1971] and perhaps others have described species of Neastacilla from places in the Northern Hemisphere. These species must be placed in other genera.

Astacilla marionensis Beddard

Astacilla marionensis Beddard, 1886, p. 107, Plate 25, fig. 5

Since Beddard [1886] named the species marionensis, it is presumed here that the illustrated specimen is from Marion Island region, not Île Kerguelen. Appendages are lacking on peraeonal segment VII for the illustrated specimen, although it is a gravid female.

Diagnosis. Body thin and cylindrical. Dorsum of peraeonal segments IV with some tubercles. Small posterolateral spines present on pleon; posterior margin drawn out to point. Anterior part (three indicated segments) of pleon much less than half total length of pleon.

Measurements. Holotype gravid female 8 mm long.

Type locality. Off Marion Island, near Île Kerguelen; Challenger (no station number); 183 m.

Distribution. Known only from type locality.

Remarks. Vanhöffen [1914] considered the two specimens that Beddard obtained from shallow water

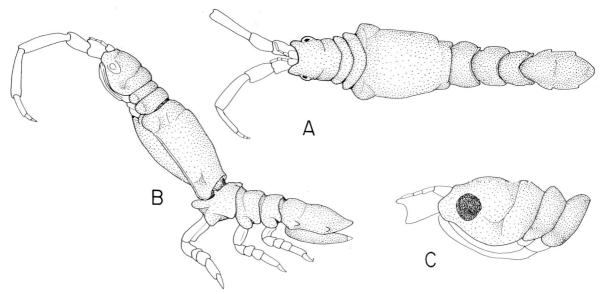

Fig. 16. Astacilla diomedeae Benedict, 1898. A, holotype gravid female 5.4 mm long; B, lateral view holotype; C, lateral view anterior part.

in Anse Betsy, Île Kerguelen, to be A. kerguelensis Vanhöffen, Beddard mentioned that they were different, although the only difference that he cited was that they were more pigmented. Tattersall [1921] regarded A. marionensis as identical to A. kerguelensis (see remarks under A. kerguelensis). It is my opinion that until specimens are examined from near Marion Island, the type locality, the species must be regarded as distinct.

Astacilla diomedeae Benedict
Figs. 16A-16C

Astacilla diomedeae Benedict, 1898, p. 50, Figure 10.--Ohlin, 1901, p. 265.--Menzies, 1962, p. 87.

The species is redescribed and re-illustrated here using the type specimen, a gravid female.

Diagnosis. Cephalon about half as wide as gravid peraeonal segment IV. Anterior corners of segment IV not extended anteriorly and lateral to segment III. Posterior margin of segment IV about as wide as anterior margin of segment V.

Redescription. (The type specimen was not dissected, so the observations of the appendages are based on attached appendages.) Eyes lateral. Dorsum of body smooth. Cephalon and peraeonal segment I fused, but recognizable. Peraeonal segment III slightly broader than II. Anterior part of segment IV widest, tapering to narrower segment V; segment V about as broad as II. Pleon narrowest where attached to peraeon; middle part widest; posterior margin broadly rounded. Pleonal segmentation slight; lateral spines on indicated segment 3 small; posterolateral spines small. Antenna 1 about as long as basal segment of antenna 2. Antenna 2 shorter than half length of body; three flagellar articles. Peraeopod I most probably without unguis on dactylus. Peraeopods II-IV much like I but longer. Peraeopods V-VII prehensile. Valves smooth.

Measurements. Holotype gravid female 5.4 mm long (USNM 20531, not the number listed by Benedict, 1898).

Type locality. Strait of Magellan; Albatross station 2774; 58°23'00"S, 68°31'30"W; 31 m.

Distribution. Known only from type locality.

Remarks. Astacilla kerguelensis Vanhöffen has been considered as a junior synonym of this species (see remarks under that species).

Astacilla estadoensis sp. nov.
Figs. 17A-17I

The species is based on one female from the intertidal zone.

Diagnosis. Laterally placed eyes, moderately large. Dorsum smooth with only indications of pleonal segments breaking smoothness. Cephalon less than half as wide as gravid peraeonal segment IV. Anterior margin of segment IV with corners rounded and extended laterally along segment III; posterior margin wider that anterior margin of segment V.

Description. Eyes moderately large, laterally placed on cephalon. Dorsum smooth. Cephalon short, less than half as wide as gravid peraeonal segment IV. Anterior margin of segment IV with corners rounded and extended laterally around III; posterior margin wider than anterior margin of segment V. Pleon with indications of segments anteriorly; indicated segment 3 wider than other parts of pleon; posterolateral corners very small;

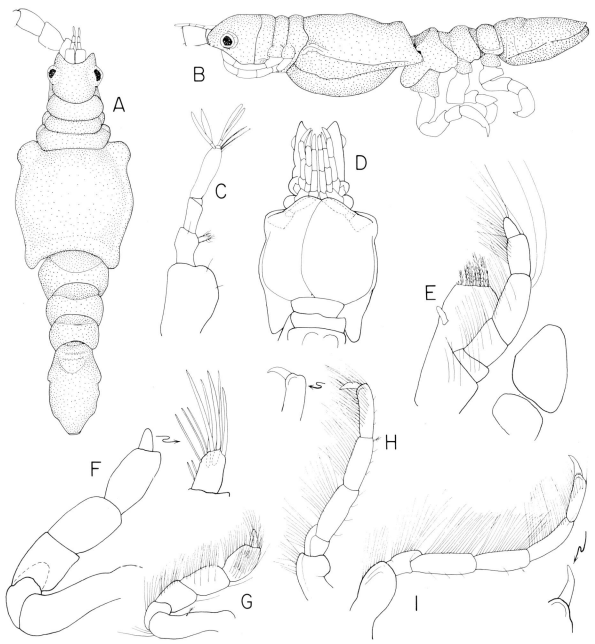

Fig. 17. *Astacilla estadoensis* sp. nov. A, holotype gravid female 6 mm long; B,
lateral view; C, antenna 1; D, ventral view anterior part; E, maxilliped; F, peraeopod
I enlarged and without setae; G, peraeopod I; H, peraeopod II; I, peraeopod III.

posterior margin narrow and more or less
truncate. Valves smooth. Body with many
melanophores.

   Antenna 1 with flagellum shorter than large
peduncular basal segment; two groups of
aesthetascs at tip. Antenna 2 broken. Maxilliped
with narrow palp, about half width of endite;
endite with one coupling hook and many setae on
sensory edge; exopod subtriangular, about half as

long as endite. Peraeopod I with small dactylus
fringed with long setae. Peraeopods II and III
with dactylus including unguis less than half
length of propodus. Peraeopod IV, proximal part
beneath marsupial covering, otherwise like II and
III. Peraeopods V-VII short and prehensile.
Valves smooth.

   Measurements. Holotype gravid female 6 mm long.
   Type locality. Isla de los Estados; Hero

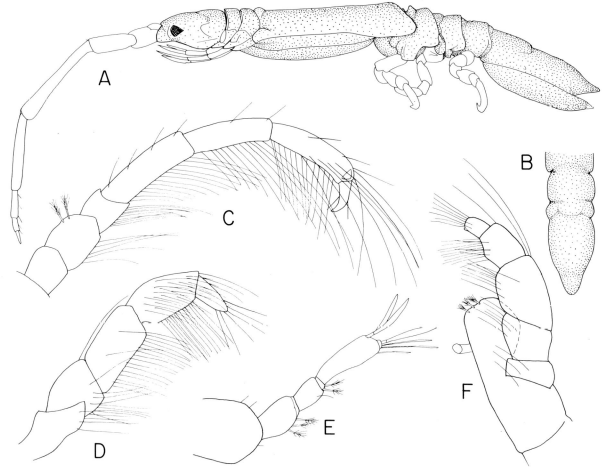

Fig. 18. _Astacilla magellanica_ Ohlin, 1901. A, lateral view gravid female 7.3 mm
long; B, dorsal view pleon; C, peraeopod II; D, peraeopod I; E, antenna 1; F,
maxilliped.

715-898; 54°50.8'S, 64°29.2'W; 54°50.8'S,
64°28.9'W; November 4, 1971; intertidal.

   Derivation of name. The name 'estadoensis'
means from Estados, the island near which the type
locality is located.

   Distribution. Known only from type locality.

   Affinities. The new species differs from _A.
diomedeae_ in having a generally rectangular
peraeonal segment IV as opposed to the posteriorly
tapered segment IV in _A. diomedeae_. It differs
from both _A. marionensis_ and _A. kerguelensis_ in
that its body is smooth and without tubercles,
among other things.

Astacilla kerguelensis Vanhöffen

Astacilla kerguelensis Vanhöffen, 1914, p. 523,
   Figure 54.--Nordenstam, 1933, p. 121.--Hale,
   1946, p. 172, Figures 5 and 6.--Kussakin, 1967,
   p. 299.
pars _Astacilla marionensis_ Beddard, 1886, p. 108

(two individuals from shallow water of Anse
Betsy, Île Kerguelen).

Additional specimens were taken by Nordenstam
[1933], Hale [1946], and Kussakin [1967] from
shallow water at Île Kerguelen. Hale [1946]
redescribed and re-illustrated the species.

   Diagnosis. Body cylindrical; tubercles, if
present, only on peraeonal segment V. Posterior
part of pleon pointed. Anterior part (three
indicated segments) only slightly less than half
total length of pleon.

   Description. See Hale [1946].

   Measurements. To 16.6 mm long.

   Type locality. Île Kerguelen; _Gauss_ station;
January 2, 1902; shallow water.

   Distribution. Île Kerguelen; shallow to 91 m.

   Affinities. The species is apparently much like
A. marionensis.

   Remarks. The reason for keeping this species
separate from _A. marionensis_ is that the body of

A. marionensis is proportionately more cylindrical and more tuberculate. Antenna 2 is proportionately elongate in A. kerguelensis. Apparently, A. kerguelensis is more strongly pigmented as well. This comparison is based on the illustrations of an 8-mm long specimen of Beddard and a 16.5-mm long specimen of Vanhöffen. Until specimens from deeper water are compared to specimens of A. kerguelensis from Anse Betsy, Île Kerguelen, the two species should be kept separate.

Astacilla magellanica Ohlin
Figs. 18A-18F

Astacilla magellanica Ohlin, 1901, p. 267, Figure 2.--Stebbing, 1914, p. 353.
Neastacilla magellanica (Ohlin).--Tattersall, 1921, p. 244.--Nordenstam, 1933, p. 122.-- Menzies, 1962, p. 87, Figures 28a-28g.

Specimens from a Hero station are redescribed here.
Diagnosis. Eyes lateral, moderately large, somewhat triangular. Cephalon and peraeonal segment I fused with little indication of fusion; peraeonal segments II and III well differentiated with pointed lateral margins.
Description. Eyes lateral, moderately large, somewhat triangular. Cephalon and peraeonal segment I fused with little indication of fusion; peraeonal segments II and III well differentiated with somewhat pointed lateral margins. Peraeonal segment IV elongate, much longer than cephalon and segments I-III combined; not much thicker at thickest part than other segments. Pleon elongate with anterior segments barely indicated and posterolateral corners absent; posterior margin produced and rounded.
Antenna 1 with short flagellum tipped with two groups of aesthetascs. Antenna 2 short and thick, shorter than body; three flagellar articles. Maxilliped with palp nearly equal in width; endite with few (about 3) setae on sensory edge; one coupling hook. Peraeopod I with dactylus supporting long setae; unguis not apparent. Dactylus on peraeopod II shorter than propodus. Dactylus of peraeopods III and IV similar. Peraeopods V-VII short and prehensile. Valves smooth. Body spotted with many melanophores. Gravid female 7.3 mm long.
Measurements. To 7.3 mm long.
Type locality. Punta Dungeness, Strait of Magellan; October 15, 1892; 18.3 m.
Distribution. The species was taken at two other stations in the Strait of Magellan--Hero 692-69-6A (the specimen redescribed here) and Lund Station 115 of Menzies [1962].
Affinities. The species is much like A. falclandica (see remarks under that species).

Astacilla falclandica Ohlin

Astacilla falclandica Ohlin, 1901, p. 266, Figure 2.--Stebbing, 1914, p. 353.--Nierstrasz, 1941, p. 256.--?Hurley, 1961, p. 264.

Neastacilla falclandica (Ohlin).--?Tattersall, 1921, p. 244, Plate 10, figs. 1-3.--Nordenstam, 1933, p. 119, Figures 28A-28C.

The species was designated as the type species of Neastacilla Tattersall [1921], but that genus is abolished and A. falclandica and A. magellanica are included in Astacilla. The species has page priority over A. magellanica if the two are ever considered to be synonyms.
Diagnosis. Eyes large. Antenna 2 long, slender, reaching to posterior margin of peraeonal segment VI.
Measurements. To 5 mm long.
Type locality. Stanley, Falkland Islands (Islas Malvinas); July 17, 1893; 1.8 m.
Affinities. The species is closely related to A. magellanica also described by Ohlin [1901].
Remarks. Stebbing [1914], who worked with specimens from the Falkland Islands, considered A. falclandica and A. magellanica to be synonyms. He did not compare specimens, and until that is done, the two species must be considered as separate. Menzies [1962] redescribed A. magellanica from the Strait of Magellan, but made no comparisons to specimens from the Falkland Islands. He considered A. magellanica to have short, thick antenna 2. Menzies also did not show the pointed margins on peraeonal segments II and III as illustrated here (Figure 18A). He also showed posterolateral corners on the pleon [Menzies, 1962, Figure 28b]. The specimens described here resemble those described by Ohlin. Until many specimens from the Falkland Islands and the Strait of Magellan are compared, A. falclandica and A. magellanica should be kept as separate species.
In my opinion Tattersall's [1921] specimens from New Zealand were not adequately described or compared to N. falclandica. Hurly [1961] noted the record of Tattersall and included the species without elaboration in his list of isopods from New Zealand as an Astacilla. The specimens from New Zealand probably represent a different species, but that requires comparison of specimens which has not been done here.

Appendix 1: Station List

R/V Eltanin

El 6.363; 57°09'S, 58°58'W; 58°00'S, 58°50'W; December 7 and 8, 1962; about 3477-3590 m. Rectarcturus tuberculatus Schultz.
EL 12-1082; 60°51'S, 42°57'W; 60°50'S, 42°59'W; April 14, 1964; 284-293 m. Dolichiscus meridionalis (Hodgson).
El 14-1192; 55°55'S, 159°52'W; 54°47'S, 159°50'W; August 6, 1964; 4187-4209 m. Paradolichiscus opiliones Schultz.
El 22-1521; 53°29'S, 52°08'W; 56°36'S, 52°18'W; January 31, 1966; 1041-1221 m. Dolichiscus meridionalis (Hodgson).
El 27-1851; 49°40'S, 178°53'W; 49°40'S, 178°54'W;

January 3, 1957; 439-540 m. Caecarcturus
quadraspinosus Schultz.
El 27-1859; 66°01'S, 176°15'E; 66°07'S, 176°18'E;
January 9, 1967; 3459-3492 m. Paradolichiscus
gaussianus (Vanhöffen).
El 27-1877; 72°18'S, 170°26'E; 72°19'S, 170°25'E;
January 15, 1967; 143-146 m. Dolichiscus
acanthaspidius Schultz.
El 27-1885; 74°30'S, 170°10'E; 74°32'S, 170°12'E;
January 16, 1967; 311-328 m. Dolichiscus
acanthaspidius Schultz.
El 27-1892; 75°27'S, 168°50'E; 75°27'S, 168°52'E;
January 18, 1967; 364-366 m. Dolichiscus
meridionalis (Hodgson).
El 27-1930; 74°19'S, 176°39'W; 74°20'S, 176°34'W;
January 28, 1967; 831-836 m. Dolichiscus
meridionalis (Hodgson).
El 27-2034; 74°32'S, 168°13'E; 74°32'S, 168°16'E;
January 18, 1967; 878-905 m. Dolichiscus
meridionalis (Hodgson).
El 32-2050; 77°01'S, 168°38'E; 77°03'S, 168°23'E;
January 22, 1968; 909-920 m. Dolichiscus
meridionalis (Hodgson).
El 32-2065; 78°23'S, 173°06'W; 78°23'S, 173°02'W;
January 26, 1968; 470-477 m. Dolichiscus
meridionalis (Hodgson).
El 32-2082; 75°50'S, 173°08'W; 75°52'S, 173°08'W;
January 31, 1968; 472-475 m. Dolichiscus
meridionalis (Hodgson).
El 32-2088; 76°58'S, 171°07'W; 76°59'S, 171°07'W;
February 2, 1968; 421-430 m. Dolichiscus
meridionalis (Hodgson).
El 32-2113; 73°19'S, 174°53'W; 73°19'S, 174°52'W;
February 9, 1968; 2897-2907 m. Dolichiscus
profundus Schultz.
El 32-2123; 72°28'S, 175°26'E; 72°26'S, 175°28'E;
December 2, 1968; 548-565 m. Dolichiscus
acanthaspidius Schultz.
El 32-2124; 71°38'S, 172°00'E; 71°38'S, 172°00'E;
December 2, 1968; 606-622 m. Dolichiscus
acanthaspidius Schultz.
El 32-2125; 71°22'S, 170°43'E; 71°22'E, 170°39'E;
February 13, 1968; 161-165 m. Dolichiscus
acanthaspidius Schultz.
El 51-5761; 76°01.48'S, 178°49.94'E; 76°01.64'S,
179°53.52'E; September 2, 1972; 388-399 m.
Dolichiscus meridionalis (Hodgson).
El 51-5762; 76°02.07'S, 179°56.98'W; 86°02.03'S,
179°52.14'W; September 2, 1972; 247-258 m.
Dolichiscus meridionalis (Hodgson), Dolichiscus
acanthaspidius Schultz.
El 51-5765; 76°07.03'S, 170°12.08'W; 76°07.45'S,
170°11.68'W; November 2, 1972; 571-587 m.
Dolichiscus meridionalis (Hodgson).

R/V Hero

H 3-29 C and G; 64°54'N, 53°38'W; August 18, 1968;
79-85 m. Arcturus baffini (Sabine),
Spectrarcturus multispinatus Schultz.
H 692-68-6A; 53°30'48"S, 70°50'33"W; April 16,
1969; 0.3-0.7 m. Astacilla magellanica Ohlin.
H 715-880; 54°50'S, 63°59'W; 54°50'S, 64°00'W;

October 28, 1971; 205-208 m. Rectarcturus
kophameli Ohlin.
H 715-898; 54°50.8'S, 64°29.2'W; 54°50.8'S,
64°28.9'W; November 4, 1971; intertidal.
Astacilla estadoensis Schultz.
H 715-903; 54°34.0'S, 64°60'W; 54°34.5'S, 64°40'W;
November 6, 1971; 84-85 m. Rectarcturus
kophameli Ohlin.
H 721-726; 62°19.3'S, 59°11.8'W; 62°19.2'S,
59°11.7'W; December 26, 1971; 64-89 m.
Dolichiscus meridionalis (Hodgson),
Cylindrarcturus elongatus Schultz.
H 721-776; 62°56.1'S, 60°49.0'W; 62°56.7'S,
60°49.6'W; January 8, 1972; 109 m. Dolichiscus
meridionalis (Hodgson).

R/V Islas Orcadas

IO 876-107; 60°26.5'S, 46°22.8'W; 60°26.5'S,
46°22.9'W; February 15 and 16, 1976; 100.5-102.4
m. Dolichiscus meridionalis (Hodgson).
IO 876-122; 61°20.2'S, 44°25.5'W; 61°20.3'S,
44°28.2'W; February 21, 1976; 274.3-285.3 m.
Acantharcturus acutipleon Schultz, Dolichiscus
diana Schultz.

Miscellaneous Stations

Balleny Islands (Buckle Island); Scripps; 66°53'S,
163°19'E; February 10, 1974; 55-146 m.
R/V Albatross station 2274; 58°23'00"S,
68°31'30"W; 31 m. Astacilla diomedeae Benedict.
Austrasian Antarctic Expedition 1914; station ii;
66°55'S, 145°21'E; 526-549 m. Paradolichiscus
debilis (Hale).
R/V Challenger station 320; 37°17'S, 53°52'W;
February 14, 1876; 1097 m. Dolichiscus anna
(Beddard).
R/V Challenger station (no station number); near
Île Kerguelen; 183 m. Astacilla marionensis
Beddard.
R/V Gauss station; Île Kerguelen; January 2, 1902;
shallow water. Astacilla kerguelensis Vanhöffen.
R/V Gauss station; east of continent--90°E, March
1, 1903; 2450 m. Paradolichiscus gaussianus
(Vanhöffen).
R/V Ob station 480; 43°40'S, 59°34'W; June 16,
1958; 399-500 m. Dolichiscus anna (Beddard).

Appendix 2

The following list of species is in the order in
which they are discussed. Asterisks indicate
specimens examined.

Arcturus Latreille, 1829
  *A. baffini (Sabine, 1824)
Spectrarcturus gen. nov.
  *S. multispinatus sp. nov.
Rectarcturus gen. nov.
  *R. kophameli (Ohlin, 1901)
  *R. tuberculatus sp. nov.
  R. patagonicus (Ohlin, 1901)

Acantharcturus gen. nov.
  *A. acutipleon sp. nov.
Dolichiscus Richardson, 1913
  D. pfefferi Richardson, 1913
  *D. meridionalis (Hodgson, 1910)
  *D. acanthaspidius sp. nov.
  D. anna (Benedict, 1886)
  *D. diana sp. nov.
Paradolichiscus gen. nov.
  *P. gaussianus (Vanhöffen, 1914)
  P. debilis (Hale, 1937)
  *P. opiliones sp. nov.
Caecarcturus gen. nov.
  *C. quadraspinosus sp. nov.
Cylindrarcturus gen. nov.
  *C. elongatus sp. nov.
Astacilla Cordiner, 1795
  A. marionensis Beddard, 1886
  *A. diomedeae Benedict, 1898
  *A. estadoensis sp. nov.
  A. kerguelensis (Vanhöffen, 1914)
  *A. magellanica Ohlin, 1901

Appendix 3: Disposition of Type Specimens

The type specimens have been deposited in the
National Museum of Natural History, Smithsonian
Institution. The numbers are United States
National Museum (USNM) numbers. The other nontype
specimens are also deposited there.

Acantharcturus acutipleon--holotype male 181252.
Astacilla estadoensis--holotype female 181256.
Caecarcturus quadraspinosus--holotype female
181257.
Cylindrarcturus elongatus--holotype female
181258.
Dolichiscus acanthaspidius--holotype female
181259.
Dolichiscus diana--holotype female 181260.
Dolichiscus profundus--holotype male 181261.
Paradolichiscus opiliones--holotype male 181262.
Recarcturus tuberculatus--holotype female 181263.
Spectarcturus multispinatus--holotype female
181264.

Acknowledgments. This work was supported for
the most part by the Smithsonian Oceanographic
Sorting Center's program 'Cooperative systematics
and analyses of the polar biological material,'
through a National Science Foundation grant DPP
76-23979, B. J. Landrum, Principal Investigator.
Special thanks is also due to the librarians of
the American Museum of Natural History.

References

Beddard, F. E.
  1886 Report on the Isopoda collected by H.M.S.
        Challenger during the years 1873-1876.
        2. Challenger Rep., 17: 1-178.
Benedict, J. E.
  1898 The Arcturidae in the U.S. National
        Museum. Proc. Biol. Soc. Wash., 12: 41-51.
Cordiner, C.
  1795 Remarkable ruins, and romantic prospects,
        of north Britain. With ancient monuments,
        and singular subjects of natural history.
        2 vols. I. and J. Taylor, London.
Gruner, H. E.
  1965 Die Tierwelt Deutschlands (und der
        angrenzenden Meeresteile nach ihren
        Merkmalen und nach ihrer Lebensweise).
        Krebstiere oder Crustaces. V. Isopoda
        (1). Gustav Fischer Verlag, Jena, 51:
        1-149.
Hale, H. M.
  1937 Isopoda and Tanaidacea. Scient. Rep.
        Australas. Antarct. Exped., Ser. C, 2(2):
        1-45.
  1946 Isopoda-Valvifera. Rep. B.A.N.Z. Antarct.
        Res. Exped., Ser. B, 5(3): 161-212.
Hansen, H. J.
  1916 Crustacea Malacostraca III. Dan. Ingolf
        Exped., 3(5): 1-262.
Hodgson, T. V.
  1910 Crustacea. Isopoda. Nat. Antarctic Exped.
        1901-1904, 5(3): 1-77.
Hurley, D. E.
  1961 A checklist and key to the Crustacea
        Isopoda of New Zealand and the
        subantarctic islands. Trans. R. Soc. N.
        Z., 1(20): 259-292.
Kensley, B.
  1975 Marine Isopoda from the continental shelf
        of South Africa. Ann. S. Afr. Mus.,
        67(4): 35-89.
Kussakin, O. G.
  1967 Fauna of isopoda and tanaidacea in the
        coastal zones of the antarctic and
        subantarctic waters. Studies of marine
        fauna IV(XII). Biol. Rep. Sov. Antarct.
        Exped. 1955-1958, 3: 220-389.
  1971 Additions to the fauna of isopods
        (Crustacea Isopoda) of the
        Kurile-Kamchatka Trench. III.
        Flabellifera and Valvifera. Explor. Fauna
        Seas, Zool. Inst. Moscow, 92: 239-273.
  1972 Isopoda from the coastal zone of the
        Kurile Islands. III. Three new arcturids
        from the middle Kuriles with taxonomic
        remarks on the family Arcturidae.
        Crustaceana, Suppl. 3, pp. 178-189.
Latreille, P. A.
  1829 Le Règne Animal distribués d'après son
        organisation, pour servir de base à
        l'histoire naturelle des animaux et
        d'introduction à l'anatomie comparée. 2nd
        ed. 4: xxvii-584S. Chez Deterville,
        Libraire, Paris.
Menzies, R. J.
  1962 The zoogeography, ecology, and systematics
        of the Chilean marine isopods. Acta Univ.
        Lund, N. F., Avd. 2, 57(11): 1-162.
Nierstrasz, H. F.
  1941 Die Isopoden der Siboga-Expedition. 4.

Isopoda Genuina. 3. Gnathiidea,
Anthuridea, Valvifera, Asellota,
Phreatoicidea. Siboga-Exped. Monogr., 32:
205-308. Brill, Leiden, Netherlands.

Nordenstam, A.
  1933 Marine Isopoda of the families Serolidae,
         Idotheidae, Pseudidotheidae, Arcturidae,
         Parasellidae and Stenetriidae mainly from
         the South Atlantic. Further Zool. Results
         Swed. Antarct. Exped., 3(1): 1-284.

Ohlin, A.
  1901 Isopoda from Tierra del Fuego and
         Patagonia. I. Valvifera. Svenska Exped.
         Magellanländerna, 2(11): 261-306.

Richardson, H.
  1905 Monograph on the isopods of North
         America. Bull. U.S. Natn. Mus., 54:
         liii-727.
  1913 Crustacés Isopodes. 2ème Expédition
         Antartique Française (1908-1910), pp.
         1-24. Masson et Cie, Paris.

Sabine, E.
  1824 Marine invertebrate animals. Supplement
         to the appendix of Capt. Parry's voyage
         1819-20. pp. 219-229. John Murray,
         London.

Schultz, G. A.
  1980 Arcturocheres gaussicola n. sp.

(Cabiropsidae) parasite on Antarcturus
gaussianus Vanhöffen (Arcturidae) from
Antarctica (Isopoda). Crustaceana, 39(2):
153-156.

Stebbing, T. R. R.
  1914 Crustacea from the Falkland Islands
         collected by Mr. Rupert Vallentin, F.L.S.
         2. Proc. Zool. Soc. London, pp. 341-378.

Tattersall, W. M.
  1921 Crustacea. 6. Tanaidacea and Isopoda.
         Nat. Hist. Rep. Br. Antarct. Terra Nova
         Exped., 8: 191-258.

Vanhöffen, E.
  1914 Die Isopoden der Deutschen
         Südpolar-Expedition 1901-1903. Dt.
         Sudpol. Exped., 15: 449-598.

White, M. C.
  1979 A new species of marine isopod of the
         genus Antarcturus (Isopoda, Valvifera)
         from the South Orkney Islands.
         Crustaceana, 36(1): 90-98.

zur Strassen, O.
  1902 Über die Gattung Arcturus und die
         Arcturiden der der Deutschen
         Tiefsee-Expedition. Zool. Anz., 25:
         682-689.
  1903 Zusatz zu meinem Artikel über die
         Arcturiden. Zool. Anz., 26: 31.

THE ANTARCTIC RESEARCH SERIES:
STATEMENT OF OBJECTIVES

The Antarctic Research Series, an outgrowth of research done in the Antarctic during the International Geophysical Year, was begun early in 1963 with a grant from the National Science Foundation to AGU. It is a book series designed to serve scientists and graduate students actively engaged in Antarctic or closely related research and others versed in the biological or physical sciences. It provides a continuing, authoritative medium for the presentation of extensive and detailed scientific research results from Antarctica, particularly the results of the United States Antarctic Research Program.

Most Antarctic research results are, and will continue to be, published in the standard disciplinary journals. However, the difficulty and expense of conducting experiments in Antarctica make it prudent to publish as fully as possible the methods, data, and results of Antarctic research projects so that the scientific community has maximum opportunity to evaluate these projects and so that full information is permanently and readily available. Thus the coverage of the subjects is expected to be more extensive than is possible in the journal literature.

The series is designed to complement Antarctic field work, much of which is in cooperative, interdisciplinary projects. The Antarctic Research Series encourages the collection of papers on specific geographic areas (such as the East Antarctic Plateau or the Weddell Sea). On the other hand, many volumes focus on particular disciplines, including marine biology, oceanology, meteorology, upper atmosphere physics, terrestrial biology, snow and ice, human adaptability, and geology.

Priorities for publication are set by the Board of Associate Editors. Preference is given to research projects funded by U.S. agencies, long manuscripts, and manscripts that are not readily publishable elsewhere in journals that reach a suitable reading audience. The series serves to emphasize the U.S. Antarctic Research Program, thus performing much the same function as the more formal expedition reports of most of the other countries with national Antarctic research programs.

The standards of scientific excellence expected for the series are maintained by the review criteria established for the AGU publications program. The Board of Associate Editors works with the individual editors of each volume to assure that the objectives of the series are met, that the best possible papers are presented, and that publication is achieved in a timely manner. Each paper is critically reviewed by two or more expert referees.

The format of the series, which breaks with the traditional hard-cover book design, provides for rapid publication as the results become available while still maintaining identification with specific topical volumes. Approved manuscripts are assigned to a volume according to the subject matter covered; the individual manuscript (or group of short manuscripts) is produced as a soft cover 'minibook' as soon as it is ready. Each minibook is numbered as part of a specific volume. When the last paper in a volume is released, the appropriate title pages, table of contents, and other prefatory matter are printed and sent to those who have standing orders to the series. The minibook series is more useful to researchers, and more satisfying to authors, than a volume that could be delayed for years waiting for all the papers to be assembled. The Board of Associate Editors can publish an entire volume at one time in hard cover when availability of all manuscripts within a short time can be guaranteed.

BOARD OF ASSOCIATE EDITORS
ANTARCTIC RESEARCH SERIES